**CUBE**
**BOOK**

WHITE STAR PUBLISHERS

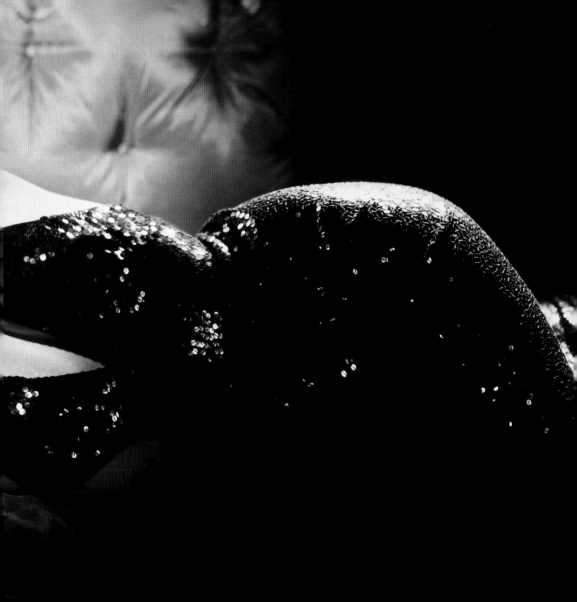

**PROJECT EDITOR**
VALERIA MANFERTO DE FABIANIS

**text**
GABRIELE BARRERA

**graphic design**
CLARA ZANOTTI

**graphic layout**
STEFANIA COSTANZO

**editorial coordination**
GIADA FRANCIA

© 2008 **WHITE STAR S.P.A.**
VIA CANDIDO SASSONE, 22-24
13100 VERCELLI - ITALY
WWW.WHITESTAR.IT

In 1982 the world is moved by the story of *E.T.*

ISBN 978-88-544-0380-2
REPRINTS:
1 2 3 4 5 6    12 11 10 09 08
Color separation: Grafotitoli, Milan.

Printed in China

# CONTENTS

## MOVIE STARS

*1* • Marilyn Monroe makes an entrance at the Actors Studio.

*2-3* • Katharine Hepburn and Spencer Tracy exchange understanding looks in *Woman of the Year*, 1942.

*4-5* • In 2002 Hugh Grant and Sandra Bullock starring in *Two Weeks Notice*.

*6-7* • Wrapped in a shape-flattering dress, Marilyn Monroe expresses all her femininity.

*8-9* • Sensual and seductive, Halle Berry lends her figure to Catwoman in the homonymous film in 2004.

*13* • Grace Kelly, future princess, in 1955 is still one of the most admired stars of Hollywood.

# Introduction

Movie star or divinity, the difference is subtle. A star was born with the French singer Edith Piaf, who made hearts weep all over world with the melody of the *"LA VIE EN ROSE."* Today, the divine movie star Marion Cotillard has been awarded an Oscar for her interpretation of Edith Piaf herself in the movie La Vie En Rose, a movie directed by Olivier Dahan. It is almost as if divinity were something contagious, infinitely replicable. What is the mechanism that creates movie stars in the third millennium? Beyond the covers of entertainment magazines,

The riveting saga of *Pirates of the Caribbean* brought fortune to Johnny Depp, one of the actors most beloved by female audiences, here in a scene from 2006.

# Introduction

ALBUM COVERS AND POSTERS, WHAT IS REAL AND AUTHENTIC AND, ON THE OTHER HAND, WHAT IS AN ARTIFICIAL CREATION OF THE FICTION FACTORY WE COMMONLY CALL CINEMA? TO ANSWER THAT, WE MUST TRY TO UNDERSTAND THE SO-CALLED STAR SYSTEM, WHICH THE 21ST CENTURY INHERITED DIRECTLY FROM THE 20TH CENTURY.

TODAY'S MOVIE STAR IS A PERSON WHO, IN PRIVATE LIFE OR IN FRONT OF AN AUDIENCE OR ON A WIDESCREEN TV, IS CAPABLE OF "BREAKING THROUGH THE SCREEN": IS THAT A TALENT OR IS IT SOMETHING THAT HAS BEEN "BUILT"? IS THAT CERTAIN MOVIE STAR, BE IT BRAD PITT OR JAMES DEAN, MARILYN MONROE OR

● A kiss that made movie history: Clark Gable as Rhett Butler, brings his face close to Vivien Leigh's, the indomitable Scarlett O'Hara, in *Gone with the Wind* (1939).

# Introduction

PENÉLOPE CRUZ, A GENUINE STAR? OR SHOULD WE BELIEVE THIS IS BUT A PROJECTION OF OUR VERY OWN DESIRES, THE FRUIT OF THE COLLECTIVE IMAGINATION OF A VAST, INTERNATIONAL, MULTIETHNIC AND HETEROGENEOUS POOL OF CINEPHILES, THAT INCLUDES ANYONE FROM THE MOVIE CRITIC TO THE BLOCKBUSTER-LOVING TEENAGER, OF WHICH ALL OF US, EVEN THOSE WHO PURCHASED THIS BOOK, ARE SOMEWHAT A PART OF? IS WHAT SHINES BEFORE US THE LIGHT OF A STAR, OR IS IT THE LIGHT OF CINEMA ITSELF (INTENDED AS SOMETHING ILLUSORY), THAT CONFOUNDS US AND ON WHICH WE REFLECT OUR OWN DESIRES?

AN EXAMPLE. AS MARCELLO MASTROIANNI MOVES

# Introduction

TOWARD THE DIVINE ANITA EKBERG IN THE INCREDI-BLY FAMOUS SCENE IN THE TREVI FOUNTAIN IN *LA DOLCE VITA,* DIRECTED BY FEDERICO FELLINI (1960), HE WHISPERS TO HER: "SILVIA, YOU ARE EVERYTHING. YOU ARE THE FIRST WOMAN ON THE FIRST DAY OF THE CREATION. YOU ARE MOTHER, SISTER, LOVER, FRIEND, ANGEL, DEVIL, EARTH, HOME." WHAT MORE? MOVIE STARS BECOME THE MOVIE ITSELF; THEY THEMSELVES BECOMES FICTION: THEY ARE NO LONGER A BODY ON A STAGE, AS IN THEATER, BUT THEY BECOME A COG IN THE ASSEMBLY LINE OF THAT DREAM FACTORY THAT, STARTING FROM THE BROTHERS LUMIÈRE TO WELLES TO ROSSELLINI TO OZU TO GODARD TO TARANTINO TO THE NEO-DISNEYAN RATATOUILLE, WE HAVE LEARNED

# Introduction

TO CALL CINEMA. A STAR LIKE ANITA EKBERG CANNOT BE EVERYTHING: SHE IS OUR IMAGINATION, OUR COLLECTIVE CINEMA SUBCONSCIOUS AND THUS BECOMES EVERYTHING, CHANGING INTO THE FACES OF CHARLIE CHAPLIN, MARLENE DIETRICH, CARY GRANT, HUMPHREY BOGART, ANNA MAGNANI, RITA HAYWORTH, AUDREY HEPBURN, MARLON BRANDO, JEAN-PAUL BELMONDO, BRIGITTE BARDOT, ROBERT REDFORD, AL PACINO, SHARON STONE AND, NOW MORE THAN EVER, SCARLETT JOHANSSON.

*21* • Paul Newman plays the part of a charming con man in *The Sting*, 1973.

*22-23* • Gary Cooper and Ingrid Bergman resting on the set of *For Whom the Bell Tolls* (1943).

*24-25* • Director J.J. Abrams directs Tom Cruise in *Mission Impossible III*, 2006.

*26-27* • In 1956 James Dean starred in *Giant*.

# FEMMES FATALES

Greta Garbo, the mysteriously fascinating Swedish actress, was nicknamed "divine."

## INTRODUCTION

CINEMA IS FEMALE. EVEN IF ITS NAME IS GENDER-NEUTRAL (IT DERIVES FROM THE ANCIENT *KÌNEMA,* OR MOVEMENT, BUT ALSO UPHEAVAL, COMMOTION), ITS REALIZATION ON THE BIG SCREEN – IN THE SPECIFIC CASES OF THE FACES OF GRETA GARBO AS WELL AS MARLENE DIETRICH, RITA HAYWORTH AND MARILYN MONROE, SOFIA LOREN AND BRIGITTE BARDOT, SHARON STONE AND NICOLE KIDMAN, CHARLIZE THERON AND ANGELINA JOLIE – IS AN EXQUISITELY FEMALE EXPRESSION. THANKS TO WOMEN CINEMA HAS REINVENTED THE CLOSE-UP AND HAS MANAGED TO HAVE THE AUDIENCE NO LONGER CONCENTRATE ON THE FULL-LENGTH OR ON THE

● Marilyn Monroe, portrayed here in the early 50s, was the sexy icon of an era.

## INTRODUCTION Femmes Fatales

HALF-LENGTH PORTRAIT – LIKE IN PRE-20TH-CEN-
TURY VISUAL ARTS, FROM PAINTING TO SCULPTURE –
BUT ON SEDUCTION: LIPS KISSING IN *THE KISS* (EDI-
SON, 1900), OR THE DISQUIETING LIGHT IN THE EX-
PRESSION OF LILLIAN GISH IN *THE LILY AND THE ROSE*
(PAUL POWELL, 1916). IN THE WORDS OF THE CRITIC
R. DYER "THE NEW MOVIE STAR LILLIAN GISH CAN BE
TAKEN AS AN EXAMPLE OF THE SEDUCTION OF EN-
TERTAINMENT" (*THE MATTER OF IMAGES: ESSAYS ON
REPRESENTATION*, 2004). HE IS RIGHT. TAKE THE ITA-
LIAN LOOK-AT-ME *FEMMES FATALES* OR DEMIGOD-
DESSES OF THE 1910S – FROM LYDA BORELLI TO
FRANCESCA BERTINI – THE AMBIGUOUS WOMEN OF
THE HOLLYWOOD OF THE 20S – FROM GRETA GARBO

## INTRODUCTION Femmes Fatales

TO THE ANDROGYNOUS MARLENE DIETRICH, "THE WOMAN THAT EVEN WOMEN CAN LOVE"; KATHARINE HEPBURN'S ICON STATUS OF *GOOD BAD GIRL* AND THE NEOCLASSICAL RITA HAYWORTH; THE NEO-REA-LISTIC, HIGH-TEMPERED ATTITUDE IN THE DRAMATIC EXPRESSION OF ANNA MAGNANI, REVIVED TODAY – AMONG OTHERS – BY THE MARVELOUS PENÉLOPE CRUZ IN *VOLVER* (ALMODÓVAR, 2006); THE STARS OF THE 50S, CHOSEN TO BECOME IMMORTAL BY HOLLY-WOOD TYPE-CASTING, MARILYN MONROE TO ELIZA-BETH TAYLOR, AND FINALLY THE BEWITCHED, BEWIT-CHING AND POTENTIALLY LETHAL WOMEN OF THE DAYS OF THE SEXUAL REVOLUTIONS, THE FASCINA-TING DOUBLES, FROM BB TO SS, AKA BRIGITTE

# Femmes Fatales
## Introduction

BARDOT AND SHARON STONE. CINEMA CAN DEFINITELY BE INTERPRETED AS A PARADE OF FASCINATING AND FIERCE FEMALES – FIGHTING IN *TIGRE REALE* (PINA MENICHELLI IN THE SAME-NAME FILM BY PASTRONE, 1916, NO LESS LETHAL THAN KATE WINSLET IN *HOLY SMOKE* ( JANE CAMPION, 1999) OR GOING AFTER THE *MATCH POINT* OF THEIR VERY OWN LIFE (SCARLETT JOHANSSON IN THE SAME-NAME FILM BY WOODY ALLEN, 2006). A *MATCH POINT* THAT THE MALE SIDE IS DESTINED TO LOSE: SOMETHING THAT, ESPECIALLY IN CINEMA, IS DEFINITELY A PLUS.

● Kim Basinger, for whom acting runs in the family, conquered international fame in the 80s with the movie *9 1/2 weeks*, from which this picture was taken.

Gloria Swanson, born in Chicago in 1898, was one of the greatest stars of the Hollywood silent era.

38 • In her long career Gloria Swanson starred in both successful dramatic
and comedic films.

39 • The charming looks and elegant style of Gloria Swanson bewitched generations
of movie lovers.

In this image, Greta Garbo wears one of the dresses used in the movie *Mata Hari* (1932). In this very successful film, Garbo plays a famous Parisian dancer who was paid to be a spy during the First World War.

Greta Garbo was born in Stockholm on 18 September 1905. Her charisma and her charm quickly made her an icon that still today is adored by film enthusiasts.

● Jean Harlow was the quintessential sex symbol of American cinema of the thirties. Because of her blonde hair, Jean Harlow is usually considered the precursor of two famous showbiz blondes: Marilyn Monroe and Madonna.

*46 and 47* ● Ruth Elizabeth Davis was nicknamed Bette by her mother, who was inspired by Balzac's novel *Cousin Bette*. Davis debuted in Broadway in the late 20s in the show *Broken Dishes*.

*48-49* ● Carole Lombard was the queen of the American screwball comedy (a sentimental type of comedy) of the 30s.

● Veronica Lake became famous in the 40s thanks to her major roles with Alan Ladd in a few *filmes noires*. Her flowing platinum hair quickly became a symbol of seduction for all women.

Graciousness, sensual charm and determination made the young Jean Harlow, portrayed here, a timeless Hollywood actress.

● Ginger Rogers lent her image to the
ads produced by the RKO production
agency in 1936. RKO produced the
musicals that gave Rogers her success
together with Fred Astaire.

● Claudette Colbert, who was French by birth only, debuted in theater in the early 30s and, after only five years, she won an Oscar as best actress.

● Marlene Dietrich's two intense expressions, with the ever-present cigarette, highlight her still-engaging charisma. Dietrich is among the most beautiful icons of 19th-century cinema

Marlene Dietrich was a famous actress and singer, a symbol of the femme fatale in an era in which divas were not allowed to show anything other than their own charm.

Marlene Dietrich, portrayed here in 1933, was born in Germany but emigrated to the United States in 1930, at the height of her career.

64 • Vivien Leigh won success with audiences in 1939, by starring in *Gone with the Wind*, from which this picture is taken.

65 • The intense stare and thick head of hair were the "brand name" of Vivien Leigh's Latin charm.

● During the course of her career, Olivia de Havilland, the beautiful actress who portrayed Melania Hamilton in *Gone with the Wind* by Victor Fleming, showed great dramatic talent along with an undisputed beauty.

Katharine Hepburn embodied feisty and mindful beauty. She obtained twelve Oscar nominations as best actress and won four.

Katharine Hepburn obtained success acting with John Barrymore in *A bill of divorcement* in 1932. From that moment on her career took off and her face became famous even on the European screens.

• Even before becoming famous in Hollywood, the English star Jeanne Simmons won great success at home, playing Ophelia in the movie *Hamlet* (1948), directed by Laurence Olivier.

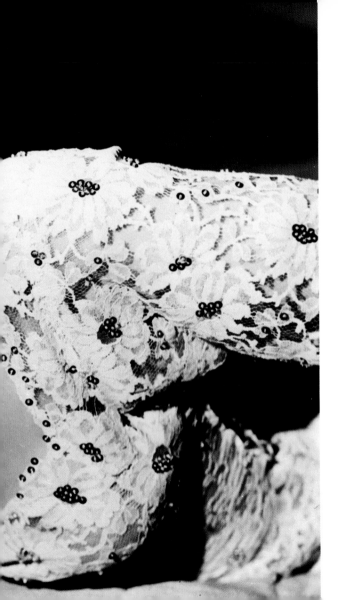

● Joan Fontaine reached the height of her notoriety between the 40s and 50s. Her career blossomed with the film *Rebecca, the first wife* directed by Alfred Hitchcock.

Two intense shots portray Joan Crawford in 1939, the year in which she played an important dramatic role in the movie *The Women,* directed by George Cukor.

● Joan Crawford received an Oscar as best actress in 1946, playing a divorced woman struggling with her daughters in the movie *Mildred Pierce*.

• During her long career as a Hollywood star, Lana Turner always played very passionate women. Her beauty opened the doors to the world of cinema at the tender age of 14, when she was noticed by a Hollywood Reporter photographer.

Lauren Bacall, born in 1924, debuted in cinema in the Howard Hawks production *To Have and Have Not* (1944). On the set she met Humphrey Bogart, with whom she fell in love.

• Lauren Bacall, nicknamed "The Look" for her beautiful eyes, starred in many films with Humphrey Bogart.

● Ingrid Bergman was awarded an Oscar. The movie *Intermezzo* by Gustaf Molander in 1936, was the movie that made her a star.

● For her entire career Rita Hayworth was associated with the character of the sexy temptress whom she played in *Gilda* (1946).

To exalt her unique charm, Rita Hayworth dyed her hair red, and became a timeless symbol of passionate love.

● Simone Signoret's unconventional charm, appreciated since the 30s, lasted until the 50s, despite the tragic break of WW II and new generations of stars in.

• Judy Garland was an actress, ballerina and a singer with great stage presence and a deep, intense voice.

• Ava Gardner played numerous roles as a true femme fatale; her charm still resonates today in movies such as *My Forbidden Past* (1951) with Robert Mitchum, from which these shots are taken.

● Ava Gardner proved she could easily balance charm and mystery, to the point where many critics defined her beauty as "nocturnal and raw."

Grace Kelly was first a model, then an actress; she debuted in 1951 in *Fourteen Hours*, when she was 22.

*102* • Gorgeous, blonde, tall and sophisticated, Grace Kelly contrasts with the Junoesque beauties of the day and becomes a main character of both male and collective admiration.

*103* • In *To Catch a Thief* (1955) Kelly's elegant beauty reached the height of its expression.

*104* • Marilyn Monroe was "America's Sweetheart" the 50s and 60s.

*105* • In *The Seven Year Itch* (1955) Monroe brought sensuality as well as a great and unexpected sense of humor.

In this picture taken in a studio in 1957, Marilyn Monroe is at the height of her beauty. Still today she is considered to be one of cinema's most fascinating women of all time.

*108 and 109* • Kim Novak portrayed on the set of *Pushover* (1954). The actress arrived in Hollywood after having traveled around America advertising a famous brand of refrigerators.

*110-111* • Audrey Hepburn arrived in Hollywood with the movie *Roman Holiday*, in which she starred alongside Gregory Peck.

Audrey Hepburn, who played Princess Anna in *Roman Holiday*, won the Oscar as best actress in 1954.

In the early 60s, Audrey Hepburn's style became a trademark, and her face began to appear in every fashion magazine.

116 ● In these images, Brigitte Bardot poses with three little hats that were specifically designed for her by the stylist Jean Barthet in 1959.

117 ● Despite being French, Bardot managed to capture the attention of the American media.

118 • Brigitte Bardot is more seductive than ever in *Love Is My Profession* (1958).

119 • Brigitte Bardot left the scene very early, in 1974. She left behind a 20-years career full of success as well as a few frustrations.

120 • Shirley MacLaine debuted in 1955 in Alfred Hitchcock's *The Trouble With Harry*.
It was an immediate success, and her unsophisticated look was loved by audiences
and critics alike.

121 • *What a Way to Go!* comes at the height of Shirley MacLaine's young career, in 1964.

122 • Julie Christie is portrayed here in a scene from *Doctor Zhivago* (1965), the movie that made her famous.

123 • Julie Christie graduated from the Central School of Speech and Drama in London and found the path to cinema was paved with success after having starred in the TV series *A for Andromeda*.

124 • Ursula Andress poses in a bikini in 1965. After her appearance in *Dr. No*, in 1962, the impresarios were haunted by her form.

125 • In 1965 Ursula Andress starred in *The 10th Victim*, with Marcello Mastroianni, taken from the Robert Sheckley novel. It was most likely the last success of her career.

• Jane Fonda came from actor stock (her father was Henry Fonda) and started her career as a star in *Tall Story* (1960); she became the director Roger Vadim's muse, who shot the unforgettable *Barbarella* (1968).

Candice Bergen, left, portrayed on the set of *The Day the Fish Came Out* (1967) and *The Group* (1967) right, debuted in 1966 but success only came later. The TV series *Murphy Brown* brought her success in the 90s: five Emmy Awards and two Golden Globes.

130 • Faye Dunaway obtained the main role in *Puzzle of a Downfall Child* (1970). From that moment, triumphant part of her career began.

131 • In 1967, in the days of *Bonnie and Clyde*, Dunaway starred alongside Warren Beatty and brought the legend of the gangster couple back to life.

132 ● *The Taming of the Shrew* (1967) marked a turning point in Taylor's professional life.

133 ● Elizabeth Taylor, debuting here in 1953, embodied the role of the diva both in front
of the camera and in real life.

- Elizabeth Taylor won an Oscar as best actress for the movies *Butterfield 8* (1960) and *Who's Afraid of Virginia Woolf?* (1966).

136 • With huge doe-eyes and a childlike look, Catherine Deneuve debuted when she was really young in 1956, but garnered her first real applauses in *The April Fools* (1969).

137 • Catherine Deneuve was beloved by directors like Polanski and Bunuel and she won a César as best actress in 1981 for *The Last Metro* by François Truffaut and in 1992 for *Indochina*.

Ann-Margret Olsson started as a singer; then, in 1961, she secured a role in *Pocketful of Miracles* by Frank Capra. In these images we see her in her debut (left) and posing for photographers in the early 70s (right).

*140, 141 and 142-143* • Sophia Loren is famous all over the world not only for her breathtaking Mediterranean beauty, but for her great dramatic and witty talent, which was awarded an Oscar in 1961 for the film *La Ciociara* (*Two Women*) by Vittorio De Sica.

*144-145* • Sigourney Weaver looks at New York's skyscrapers from her apartment window in 1979.

*146 and 147* • The delicate features of Michelle Pfeiffer express both fragility and inner strength, characteristics that are common to many of her characters.

• After having obtained success when
she was barely fourteen with the 1980
cult movie *La Boum (The Party)* the
French actress Sophie Marceau has
alternated dramatic roles with romantic
roles in costume.

In 1967 the film *One Million Years B.C.* gives the American actress Raquel Welch international fame and turns her into the decade's sex-symbol.

The glossy *9 1/2 Weeks* by Adrian Lyne in 1986 gives the world the beauty and sensuality of Kim Basinger.

Jacqueline Bisset, pictured here in the early 1970s, quickly becomes an icon of fashion that is always elegant and never vulgar.

The daughter of actors, Melanie Griffith was used to being on the scene as a child, and the audience got to know her especially for her role as the ambitious and sexy character in *Working Girl* (1988).

158 • Renée Zellweger is known to audiences mainly for her extraordinary chameleonic qualities: from the plump Bridget Jones, in the film of the same name (2001), to the sexy star of *Chicago* (2002).

159 • Sweetness and intensity are evident on the face of Naomi Watts, shown here on the set of *King Kong* (2005).

Nicole Kidman has often alternated complex roles in art films with roles in blockbusters such as *The Golden Compass*, 2007.

In 1992, two years after she had attracted attention in the action movie *Total Recall*, on the right, Sharon Stone starred in the scandalous thriller *Basic Instinct*, making her part of the history of cinema and transforming her into the sex symbol of an era.

• Demi Moore's career, which skyrocketed in 1990 with the romantic *Ghost*, takes a decisive turn towards more sexy and scandalous roles in 1996, with *Striptease*, right.

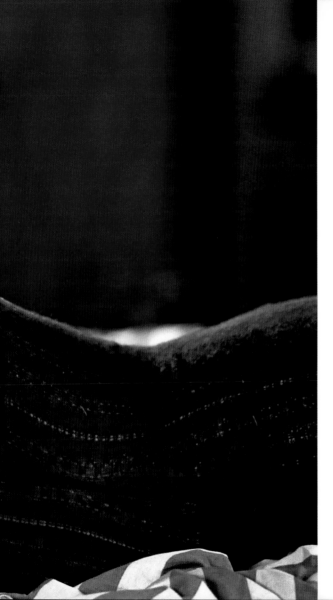

● Even though Monica Bellucci lives and works mainly in France, she is considered the symbol of Italian beauty throughout the world.

Juliette Binoche's acting intensity, her beauty and her ability to alternate small productions with huge blockbusters have made her one of the most appreciated and famous actresses of both French and international cinema.

• Since when she was young, Uma Thurman has asserted herself as a versatile and eclectic actress: once she left romantic roles in costume behind, she became the muse of director Quentin Tarantino, with whom she shot the cult movie *Kill Bill* in 2003, left.

● Cameron Diaz is famous not just for her passionate, unsophisticated beauty, but for her likeability, her strong character and the exuberance comes through in her performances.

• The provocative beauty and outrageous personality of Angelina Jolie load each character portrayed by the actress with a strong sensuality, like in *Mr. & Mrs. Smith*, 2005 and *Tomb Raider*, 2001.

The former child prodigy Kirsten Dunst managed to transform herself in one of the most appreciated young promises of American cinema.

Cate Blanchett's acting is characterized by class and charisma, whether she is portraying the austere queen of England, such as in *Elizabeth: The Golden Age*, 2007, right, or the passionate Charlotte Gray, left, in the homonymous film of 2002.

● Cate Blanchett faces the photographers on the red carpet at the Berlin International Film Festival in 2007.

• Of all the movies that made Catherine Zeta-Jones famous, two stand out: *The Mask of Zorro*, 1998, and *Chicago*, the 2001 movie that gave her an Oscar as best supporting actress.

She has been compared to Audrey Hepburn for her class and elegance,
to Lucille Ball for her comedic verve and to Bambi for her sweetness. What seems
certain is that Julia Roberts is one of the most famous and beloved actresses of all times.

• Romantic period costumes worn by Keira Knightley in many of her movies, such as *Atonement*, 2007, left and *Pride and Prejudice*, 2005, right, do not soften the determination and artistic maturity of one of the most promising young actresses.

● Penélope Cruz managed to conquer Hollywood with the sensuality of her Latin charm, which she expresses especially when directed by Spanish directors such as in *The Girl of Your Dreams*, 1998, left, and *Volver* by Pedro Almodóvar, 2006, right.

It is certainly not by chance that a young emerging actress such as Scarlett Johansson is the inspiring muse to a character of the caliber of Woody Allen: it simply means that a new diva is born.

The delicate beauty of Natalie Portman contains a strong and reserved character that has protected her from the scandals of the star system and has guided her in choosing complex roles such as in *Closer*, 2004, left, and *V for Vendetta*, 2005, right.

● Her extraordinary acting perfection transformed Meryl Streep into a living movie legend.
Her charisma easily manages both art films and comedies such as
*The Devil Wears Prada*, 2006, left.

Charlize Theron has proven she is not only one of the world's most beautiful women, but also a charismatic actress.

198 • The erotic power that made Charlize Theron famous transpires in this image, taken from the sci-fi movie *Aeon Flux*, 2005.

199 • Born in South Africa, and American by adoption, Theron is considered the heir to the stars of the Sixties.

● Playful moments
in a career chock full
of movies, even serious
ones. *Batman – The
Return* (1992) showed
a sinuous and sensual
Michelle Pfeiffer playing
the character of
Catwoman.

● Strong and fragile, beautiful and feisty, the women played by Michelle Pfeiffer fit her perfectly: like the evil witch in *Stardust*, a fantasy film from 2007.

• In 2003 the seductive British actress Kate Beckinsale conquers Hollywood once and for all by playing vampire with a heart of gold in *Underworld* .

The "black Venus" of Hollywood, Halle Berry, will surely be remembered in movie history for being the first black woman to win an Oscar as best actress.

ON the SET

Audrey Hepburn and Gregory Peck on the set of *Roman Holiday* (1953).

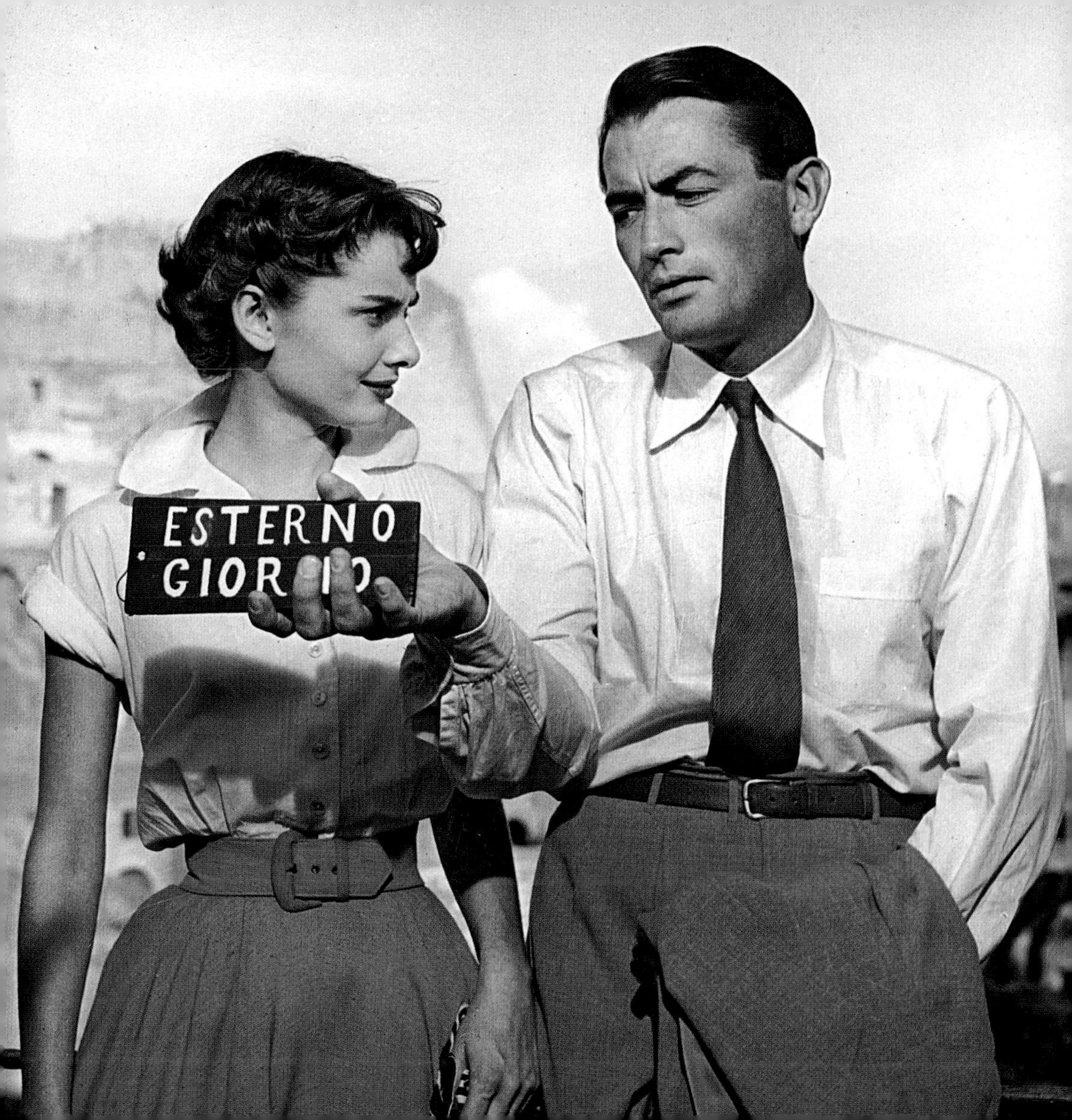
ESTERNO

## INTRODUCTION On the Set

An anonymous street, an anonymous city, an anonymous studio (probably the *black maria*) in one of the many American states (New Jersey). 7 January 1894. Thomas Alva Edison – the inventor of the light bulb himself – calls an employee in front of his machine, the kinetoscope. "Come here, Sancho Panza," he calls him à la Don Quixote. The employee's name is Fred Ott, and Edison asks him to sneeze in front of the kinetoscope. He is the first actor on a set in the history of cinema (*before* cinema can be considered born, before its official birth with the Lumière cinématographe in Paris in 1895). As a "first-time actor," like all stars all over the world, Fred Ott is amused by where he is, as he hints to

Sean Connery and Jill St. John joking around while filming *Diamonds Are Forever*, 1971.

# INTRODUCTION On the Set

DICKSON THE OPERATOR, REVEALING THE SET-ACTOR COMPLICITY IN THE SIMPLE PERFORMANCE OF A SNEEZE. THE PLACE IS LOWLY, LOWLY IS THE HANDKERCHIEF THAT OTT HOLDS IN HIS HAND AND WHICH HE *NEVER* USES. A JOURNALIST – REVIEWING *THE SNEEZE* IN *HARPER'S WEEKLY* – WRITES THAT "THE ILLUSION IS INCREDIBLE, THE ACTOR IS SO COMFORTABLE ON THE SET, THAT WE FEEL LIKE SAYING GOD BLESS YOU!" FROM THAT MOMENT ON, THE ATMOSPHERE THAT ACTORS LIVE IN ON THE SET WILL SOMEHOW END UP ON FILM, MORE OR LESS ADULTERATED: LIKE KIRK DOUGLAS WITH HIS CARAVAN MADE FOR LOVE ENCOUNTERS ON THE SET OF STANLEY KUBRICK'S *SPARTACUS* (1960); OR THE SET OF THE WERNER HERZOG FILM WITH FIGHTS AND GUNSHOTS WITH THE ACTOR KLAUS KINSKI; OR THE SET OF *ROME OPEN CITY* WITH ROBERTO ROSSELLINI (1945) WHO

# INTRODUCTION On the Set

WENT TO CAFÉS WHILE HIS PARTNER ANNA MAGNANI TRIPPED DURING THE MAIN SCENE OF THE MOVIE.

ANOTHER EXAMPLE OF THE MUTUAL RELATIONSHIP BETWEEN LOCATION AND ACTOR? THE LOCATIONS OF LUCHINO VISCONTI'S *OBSESSION* (1943), *STROMBOLI* (ROBERTO ROSSELLINI, 1949) AND *RESPIRO* (EMANUELE CRIALESE, 2001), IN WHICH SET DESIGNS REFLECT ONTO THE PHYSICALITY OF THE MAIN FEMALE PROTAGONISTS: CLARA CALAMAI, INGRID BERGMAN, VALERIA GOLINO. THE VIVID COLORS OF THE SET OF GENE KELLY AND DEBBIE REYNOLDS IN *SINGING IN THE RAIN,* BY KELLY AND DONEN (1952), DIRECTLY INFLUENCE THE DANCE. AND IN UNNATURAL LOCATIONS, LIKE IN *TERMINATOR 2* OR *TITANIC* BY JAMES CAMERON (RESPECTIVELY 1991 AND 1997), THE ICINESS OF THE MACHINES, CYBORGS OR TRANSATLANTIC, SEEM TO

# On the Set
## Introduction

BLEND PERFECTLY WITH THE ACTORS, BE IT ARNOLD SCHWARZENEGGER OR LEONARDO DICAPRIO. IN SOME CASES, HISTORY RECORDS BONA FIDE "FATAL ATTRACTIONS": BY ACTING IN THE DESERT, IN SECRET BASES FOR ATOMIC EXPERIMENTS, MANY MOVIE STARS WHO ACTED IN WESTERNS CONTRACTED CANCER. AND WHAT ABOUT THE CRAZY LOCATION WHERE ELIZABETH TAYLOR WAS *CLEOPATRA* (JOSEPH MANCKIEWICZ, 1963)? PERHAPS A PREMONITION OF THE ACTRESS'S FLOP. WHAT IS CERTAIN IS THAT THE LOCATIONS WHERE THE MOST FAMOUS MOVIES WERE SHOT ARE STILL IMPRESSED IN THE COLLECTIVE CONSCIOUSNESS AS MUCH AS THEY ARE IN THE FACES OF THE MAIN CHARACTERS.

*215* • Paul Newman resting after shooting a scene in *Cool Hand Luke* (1967).

*216-217* • Stan Laurel and Oliver Hardy fool around with the camera.

Katharine Hepburn relaxing with other actors on the set of *Sea of Grass* (1947). The film takes place in New Mexico in 1880.

220 • Brigitte Bardot in a bikini walking her dog in 1957.

221 • Humphrey Bogart has fun taking pictures of his dog Scottie.

222 • Katharine Hepburn reads some magazines, looking for comments about her.

223 • Groucho Marx strikes a funny pose in a photograph taken in 1955.

224 • Doris Day jokes around with her second husband and producer Martin Melcher, 1957.

225 • James Cagney lifts Bette Davis, who stars in *The Bride Came C.O.D.* (1941).

226 • Clark Gable reads the novel that inspired the film *Gone with the Wind* (1939), in which
he played the role of Rhett Butler.

227 • Gary Cooper in costume reading *A Farewell to Arms* by Hemingway while filming the
homonymous 1932 movie.

Gary Cooper, Ingrid Bergman and the director Sam Wood go over the parts while filming *For Whom the Bell Tolls* (1943).

230 • Anthony Quinn enjoys a break from filming and plays with his son.

231 • Fred Astaire and his son play around on the set of the 1948 musical *Easter Parade*.

● Montgomery Clift and Elizabeth Taylor chatting on the set of *A Place in the Sun* (1951). The two actors of *A Place in the Sun*, right, at Paramount Studios, were good friends.

234 ● John Wayne's son acts like his dad on the set of *War Wagon* (1967).

235 ● John Wayne's daughter starring next to her father in *Donovan's Reef* (1963).

236 • The final touch on Audrey Hepburn's make-up before entering the scene in *Sabrina*, 1954.

237 • Marilyn Monroe portrayed while she puts on her make-up on the set of *Clash by Night* (1952).

*238-239* • Audrey Hepburn falls asleep while reading a script.

*239* • Marilyn Monroe uses a truck to rest on the set of *River of No Return* (1954).

● Sophia Loren has her measurements taken by tailors and costume designers before filming *The Pride and the Passion* (1957).

*242* • Katharine Hepburn on the set of *Long Day's Journey into Night*, a 1962 drama.

*243* • Doris Dowling goes over her part in *Bitter Rice* (1950).

*244-245* • Lauren Bacall checks Humphrey Bogart's make-up on the set of
*The African Queen*, 1951.

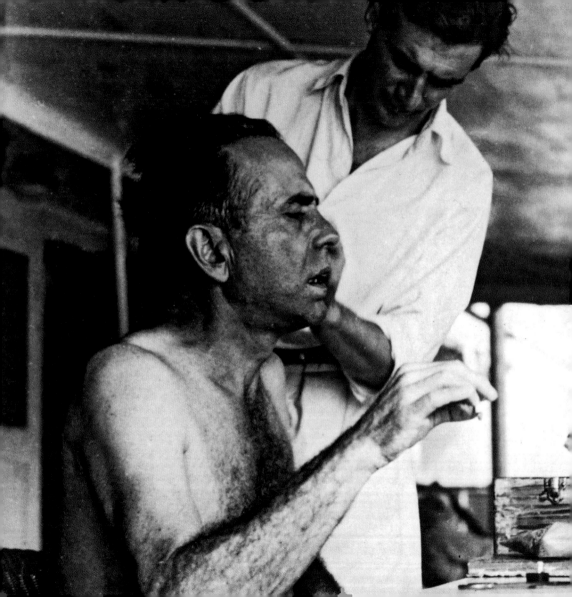

246 ● Rita Hayworth has some problems with her dress while playing the role of Gilda in the 1946 film with the same name.

247 ● A zealous costume designer fixes James Dean's shirt on the set of *Rebel Without a Cause* (1955).

248 • Marlene Dietrich relaxing during the production of the western movie
*Destry Rides Again* (1939).

249 • Marilyn Monroe and Jane Russell waiting to pose for the advertising of
*Gentlemen Prefer Blondes* (1953).

250 • Grace Kelly and James Stewart with a dog in 1954.

251 • Audrey Hepburn and Gregory Peck play cards on the set of *Roman Holiday* (1953).

252 • Marlon Brando (Mark Antony) and Louis Calhern (Caesar) during a friendly chat on the set of *Julius Caesar* (1953).

253 • Marlon Brando, in the role of Mark Antony in *Julius Caesar (1953)*, getting a drink.

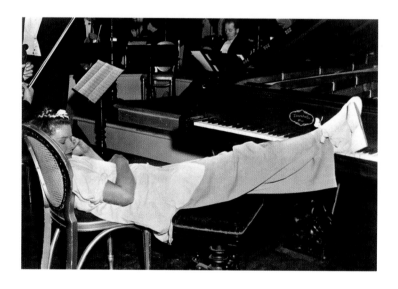

254 • Katharine Hepburn, exhausted from filming, sleeps on a piano.

255 • Gary Cooper allows himself a pleasant rest under the shade of a tree, after filming a scene in the movie *Samoa* (1953).

256 • Gregory Peck smokes while looking at the set of *Captain Newman* (1963).

257 • Glenn Ford smokes a pipe and looks at the set of *Gallant Journey* (1946).

Ava Gardner and Grace Kelly talking to some inhabitants of Tanganyika during the production of *Mogambo* (1953).

260 ● Ava Gardner during a break in filming *Knights of the Round Table* (1953).

261 ● Ava Gardner does not give up primping even on the "exotic" set of *Mogambo*.

262 ● Jean Paul Belmondo's little dog uses his owner's chair.

263 ● Elizabeth Taylor plays with a cat, from her dressing room on the set of *The Girl Who Had Everything* (1953).

264 • Grace Kelly pretends to shave director Alfred Hitchcock on the set of *To Catch a Thief* (1955).

265 • Make-up artists take care of Grace Kelly's face before filming *High Society* (1956).

266 ● Elizabeth Taylor looking like a queen even when not wearing the sumptuous costumes of *Cleopatra* (1963)

267 ● The 1956 film *Giant* takes place in Texas, and stars James Dean and Elizabeth Taylor.

268-269 ● Gregory Peck and Ava Gardner on a break while filming *On the beach* (1959).

*270-271* ● Elizabeth Taylor completes the make-up of the Egyptian queen as her son and a little actor watch on the set of the blockbuster *Cleopatra* (1963).

*272-273* ● Gloria Grahame gives her son her seat on the set of *The Man Who Never Was* (1956).

274 • Audrey Hepburn in costume plays golf with John Huston, the director of *The Unforgiven* (1960).

275 • Billy Wilder, director of *Some like It Hot* (1959), shows Jack Lemmon how to act the next scene.

276 • It's 1959 and Ben Hur (Charlton Heston) after using a chariot, rides a motorcycle.

277 • Charlton Heston concentrated on reading despite the heavy costumes for the movie
*El Cid* (1961).

*278* • Marilyn Monroe hugs Eli Wallach, her partner in *The Misfits* (1960).

*279* • The actors from *The Misfits* tease the female protagonist: Marilyn Monroe.

*280-281* • Marilyn Monroe takes any opportunity she can to rest on the set of *The Misfits*.

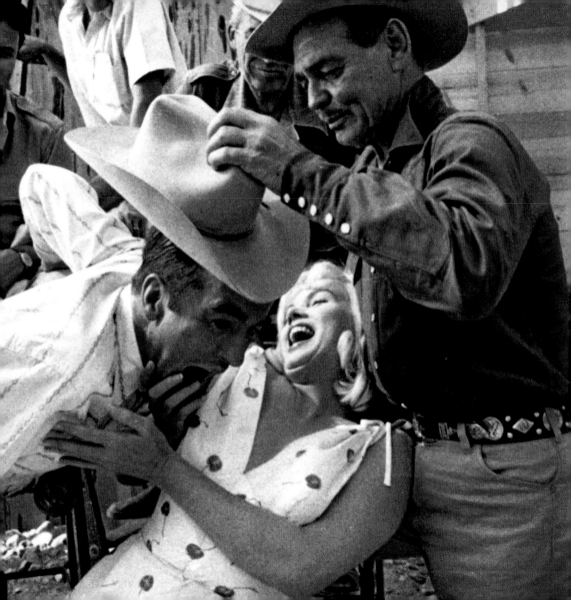

*282* • Joan Crawford's face expresses the difficulty involved in learning her part for *The Best of Everything* (1959).

*283* • Clark Gable goes over his character's lines in *The Misfits*.

*284-285* • Marlon Brando takes pictures of some Polynesians during the production of *The Mutiny on The Bounty* (1962).

• Outdoors or on a break on the set of *A Streetcar Named Desire*, right, Marlon Brando studies the script he has to play in a recording studio.

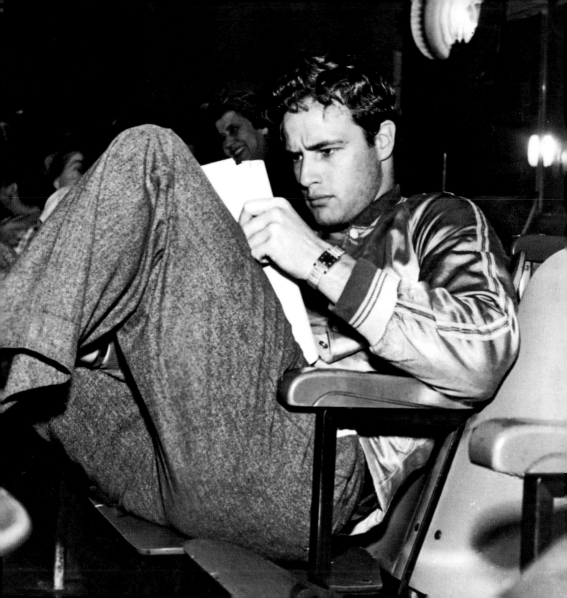

288 • Marlon Brando has just shot a scene for *The Nightcomers* (1972) and hasn't yet removed his make-up.

289 • Karl Malden pulls a prank Marlon Brando on the set of *One-Eyed Jacks* (1961).

Relaxed and meditative, Brigitte Bardot takes a break while filming *A Very Private Affair* (1962).

Sean Connery and Ursula Andress have fun and play on the beach where they are filming *Dr. No* (1962).

294 • Grace Kelly and Clark Gable get acquainted with a little Kenyan girl between scenes of the film *Mogambo* (1953).

295 • Sean Connery signs a coconut for a little Jamaican girl on the set of *Dr. No*.

296-297 • Federico Fellini tells an actress what expression to use in a scene they are filming for *8 1/2* (1963).

298 • Peter O'Toole as Lawrence of Arabia, writing a letter.

299 • Peter O'Toole as Lawrence of Arabia, resting away from the grind and the heat, leaning on a dromedary.

*300* • Peter O'Toole adlibs an improbable conversation with a dromedary.

*301* • Clint Eastwood and George Kennedy play with a cow during a break from filming for *The Eiger Sanction* (1975).

Gregory Peck rests like a real cowboy after filming *Duel in the Sun* (1946).

304 • Julie Andrews finishes putting on makeup for her role as Maria the housekeeper in the musical *The Sound of Music* (1965).

305 • James Stewart checks his make-up in a mirror before going on stage of *Flight of the Phoenix* (1965).

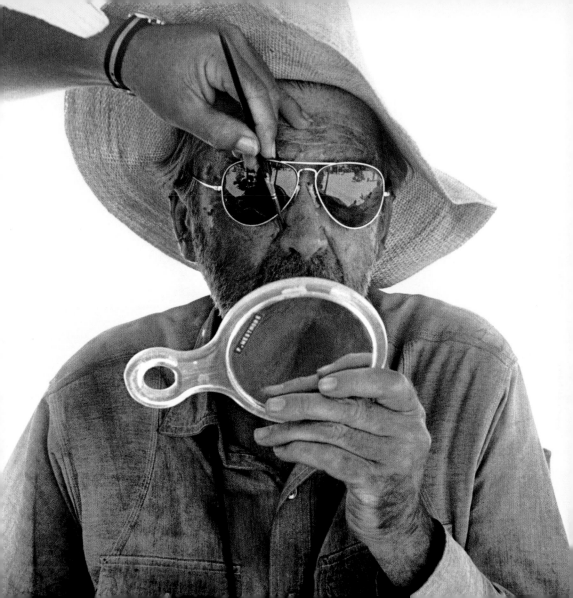

306-307 • On the set of *Planet of the Apes* (1968) there is no lack of unusual pairings.

307 • An actor dressed as an ape takes a picture of Charlton Heston.

308-309 • The stars of the western movie *The Magnificent Seven* busy (1960) pose on the street of the Mexican village where the movie takes place.

A demanding poker hand preoccupies the actors starring in *The Magnificent Seven* (1960).

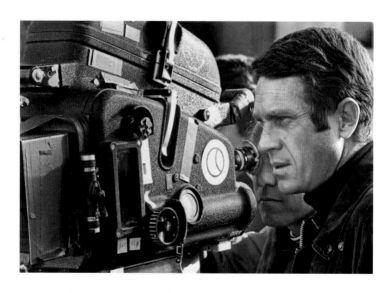

*312* • Steve McQueen sits in on shooting a scene for *Bullitt* (1968).

*313* • Sean Connery, as a Berber brigand, commands a shot while filming *The Wind and the Lion* (1975).

314 ● Joshua Lang, director of *Paint Your Wagon* (1969), sits with the actors: Clint Eastwood and Jean Seberg.

315 ● Shirley MacLaine and Clint Eastwood wait for their signal to act in *Two Mules for Sister Sara* (1970).

*316* • Meg Ryan follows preparations for *French Kiss* (1995).

*317* • Clint Eastwood tries to concentrate before acting in a scene from the western film *Two Mules for Sister Sara* (1970).

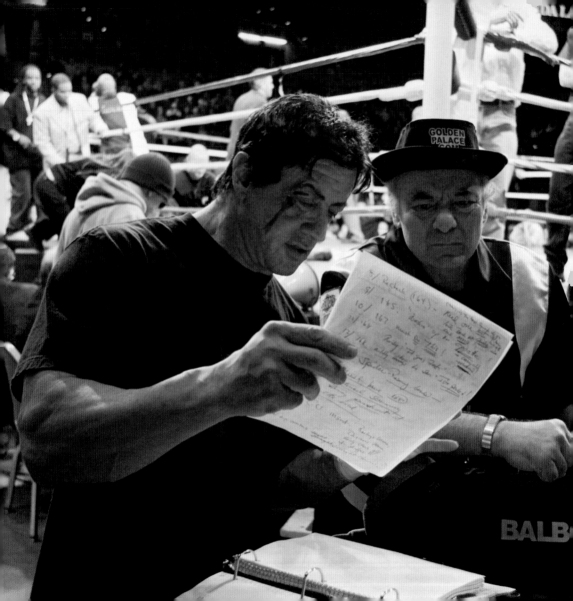

*318-319* • Sylvester Stallone comes back to the role that made him famous in *Rocky Balboa* (2006).

*319* • Sylvester Stallone, with his character's face marks, lifting a camera.

Kevin Costner, in costume, checks the shot while filming *Dances with Wolves* (1990).

*322* ● Julia Roberts checks a shot from *Hook* (1991) with Steven Spielberg.

*323* ● Julia Roberts discusses her role of Tinkerbell with Spielberg.

324 • Robert Redford and Meryl Streep confront each other on the set
of *Out of Africa* (1985).

325 • Clint Eastwood and Meryl Streep look at some pictures during a pause in the
production of *The Bridges of Madison County* (1995).

George Clooney is amused at what is happening behind him before going on set for *One Fine Day* (1996).

● Standing in the water, James Cameron gives his last directions to Kate Winslet and Leonardo DiCaprio, while filming *Titanic* (1997).

Eddie Murphy and Robert De Niro acting together in *Showtime* (2001).

*332* ● Bernardo Bertolucci jokes with the actor who plays the little emperor in
*The last emperor* (1987).

*333* ● Roberto Benigni directs little Giorgio Cantarini on how to move on the set of
*Life is beautiful* (1997).

*334* • Keira Knightley waits for action in *Pride and Prejudice* (2005).

*334-335* • Hugh Jackman is ready to shoot an arrow for a scene in *Van Helsing* (2004).

*336* ● Brad Pitt is about to enter the scene playing the hero Achilles in *Troy* (2004).

*337* ● Orlando Bloom (Paris), at the gates of Troy, waiting for action to face the Greeks.

*338-339* • Steven Spielberg assists Kate Capshaw while producing a scene from *Indiana Jones and the Temple of Doom* (1984).

*340-341* • Mel Gibson, director of *Apocalypto* (2006), personally helps in shooting a scene of a river crossing.

*342* • The director of *Die Another Day* (2002) gives the last directions to the protagonist, Pierce Brosnan.

*343* • Gabriele Muccino explains a scene to Will Smith, lead role in the movie *The Pursuit of Happiness* (2006).

Kirsten Dunst in 2006 playing Marie Antoinette for Sophia Coppola.

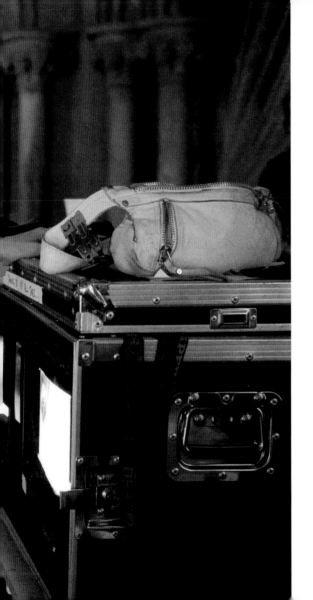

*346-347* • Cate Blanchett following the production of *Elizabeth - The Golden Age* (2007).

*347* • Long white dress and short hair, Cate Blanchett begins playing Queen Elizabeth I of England.

348-349 • The actors' costumes are fixed up before filming a scene in *Pirates of the Caribbean: At World's End* (2007).

350-351 • The operator closely follows Johnny Depp's movements in the water as captain Jack Sparrow in *Pirates of the Caribbean: The Curse of the Black Pearl* (2003).

# The TOUGH·GUY SCHOOL

- Rebel Without a Cause: the trademark of Marlon Brando, class of 1924, portrayed here in 1951.

# **INTRODUCTION** The Tough-Guy School

IF CINEMA IS A FEMALE MACHINE, AS MENTIONED BEFORE, MALE CHARACTERS THROUGHOUT THE HISTORY OF CINEMA ARE EQUALLY SHINING; HEROES TO ADORE OR IN WHICH TO IDENTIFY OURSELVES, DIVINITIES OF THE TEMPLE OF THE COLLECTIVE CONSCIOUSNESS. TOUGH, FASCINATING MEN: FROM THE ICY CLINT EASTWOOD OF *THE UNFORGIVEN,* DIRECTED ONCE AGAIN BY THE FORMER WESTERN GUNMAN OF THE SERGIO LEONE FILMS, TO THE RIGID ALAIN DELON IN *THE SAMURAI* (JEAN-PIERRE MELVILLE, 1967); FROM THE REBELLIOUS JAMES DEAN IN *REBEL WITHOUT A CAUSE* (NICHOLAS RAY, 1955),

Sean Connery in *Highlander II: The Quickening* (1991). Connery is a cyclical presence on the big screen, and always manages to live new seasons.

## INTRODUCTION The Tough-Guy School

TO THE FIST-THROWING REBEL SYLVESTER STALLONE IN *ROCKY* (JOHN G. AVILDSEN, 1976); FROM THE DAZ-ZLING AND DANGEROUSLY SUPERFICIAL MARCELLO MASTROIANNI IN *LA DOLCE VITA* (FEDERICO FELLINI, 1960), TO THE DEEP *HEART-OF-DARKNESS* OF MAR-LON BRANDO IN *APOCALYPSE NOW* (FRANCIS FORD COPPOLA, 1979). VIRILE YET IRONIC, CAPABLE OF STRONG MANNERS AS WELL AS DELICATE TENDER-NESS: THE FACES HAVE CHANGED BUT THE CLICHÉ IS THE SAME, FROM STEVE MCQUEEN TO GEORGE CLOONEY, ROBERT REDFORD TO BRAD PITT, SEAN CONNERY TO HARRISON FORD. TIME, SOCIETY AND ENVIRONMENTS CHANGE. THIS IS THE RULE OF CINE-MA: MALE HEROES OFTEN RECYCLE THE SAME

## INTRODUCTION The Tough-Guy School

"MASK." BESIDES, THE INTENSITY OF EXPRESSION IS TYPICAL OF MEN FROM THE HARD-BOILED SCHOOL, THE "TOUGH-GUY SCHOOL." AN EXAMPLE IS THE HEROIC ICON OF HUMPHREY BOGART, WHO WOULD HAVE BEEN A HEMINGWAY FAVORITE: STERN AND RO-MANTIC IN *CASABLANCA* (MICHAEL CURTIZ, 1942); RIGID AND LETHAL IN *THE DESPERATE HOURS* (WILLIAM WYLER, 1955). BOGART IS THE FILM-MAN PAR EXCELLENCE: HIS FIXED EXPRESSION SUGGESTS A VOLCANIC INNER DIMENSION, WITHOUT EVER SHOWING IT. IN MALE CINEMA, IN FACT, EVERYTHING MUST REMAIN STATIC, EVEN IF EVERYTHING BLENDS AND MOVES. DELINQUENT CHARACTERS FLOW BACK IN INVESTIGATIVE ONES, THE HEROIC-ADVENTUROUS

# The Tough-Guy School

ONES INTO THE CITY-JUNGLE KIND: ROBERT DE NIRO AND CLINT EASTWOOD ARE AS MUTABLE AS THEY ARE TRUE TO THEMSELVES; YEARS BEFORE, IT WAS ERROL FLYNN OR JOHN WAYNE. THIS IS THE PARADOX OF HEROIC CINEMA IN THE MALE FORM: THE MORE ACTION, THE MORE SOLID, ROCK-LIKE MEN ARE NECESSARY. FROM KIRK DOUGLAS TO MICHAEL DOUGLAS, WITH THE SAME HEREDITARY AGGRESSIVE JAW; FROM JEAN PAUL BELMONDO TO PAUL NEWMAN; FROM RUSSELL CROWE TO BRUCE WILLIS; FROM KEANU REEVES TO JOHNNY DEPP: A SINGLE FACE FOR ALL SEASONS.

- Brad Pitt was consecrated as a superstar with the film *Seven* (1995), but his dazzling career began four years earlier with *Thelma & Louise*.

• A shameless charisma is the hallmark of Clark Gable, a model for many. Right, Rhett in *Gone With the Wind*, in 1939, inheriting Gary Cooper's part.

Tyrone Power, the quintessential "handsome man", is the epitome of the Hollywood actor, elegant, cultured and devoted to ruining his life.

*364* • Cary Grant poses for the launch of *Dream Wife*, by Sidney Sheldon, 1953.

*365* • Gary Cooper: his dream was to draw, but he became the star of over 100 films and won 2 Oscars.

● Gary Cooper in two portraits from 1931: only a few years since his debut in 1924, Gary Cooper is an accomplished actor, but there are still nine years until his consecration with his first Oscar for *High Noon*.

The hero of the 30s and 40s, Errol Flynn created adventurous characters that still today have something to give the audience.

In 1999, the protective divinity of the "tough-guy" category, Humphrey Bogart (portrayed here in 1938 and in 1939) posthumously earns the award as best male star in history.

Gregory Peck has the *physique du role* for romantic movies, but his many characters are highly dramatic: for example the unforgettable Ahab in *Moby Dick*, from 1956.

Gregory Peck in 1946: these are the fateful days of *Duel in the Sun*, where he plays an evil character, tough-guy Lewt; this is not his best role, but the movie is legendary.

*376* • Burt Lancaster during the days of the movie *The Leopard* (1963): his career begins at age 33, rather late for an actor.

*377* • Burt Lancaster, in *Kiss the Blood Off My Hands*, 1948; where he plays a murderer on the run.

*378* • Richard Burton, 1960. The son of a miner, Burton is tough in life and on the screen.

*379* • Charlton Heston, class of 1924, is the blockbuster actor of *The Ten Commandments* (1956).

● 1951, Marlon Brando fresh from his debut one year earlier in *The Men*. The second post-war period is a time of rebels, and the indomitable Brando stars in *The Wild One* (1954).

A man who does not forgive a confrontation: rock-like Brando in *The Appaloosa* (1966).

A neo-realist anti-hero, Marcello Mastroianni is a multifaceted actor, comfortable in comedies and dramas alike; he is also photogenic, with a very personable appeal.

• James Dean in *Giant* (1956), left and in *Rebel Without A Cause* (1955), right, is the prototype of the "live fast, die young" kind of hero, which will be tragically popular in the 60s and 70s.

388 • Kirk Douglas in the days of *Two Weeks in Another Town* (1962), where his part, ironically, is that of a washed-up actor.

389 • The mixed Irish-Mexican blood is a winning factor for Anthony Quinn, here in 1957.

● The hardy fighter John Wayne, left, in *Hondo* (1953) and right, in *Jet Pilot* (1957) is the film icon of an America often at war.

392 • Henry Fonda debuts in 1935 and works until his second-to-last year of life, in 1981.

393 • A real action man, James Stewart is also a brigade general, here in *The FBI Story* (1959).

● James Stewart,
nominated for five
Oscars, became a
movie icon thanks to
his versatility in a large
number of movie
genres.

396 • Yul Brynner in *The Magnificent Seven* (1960), a movie based on the values of honor, male friendship and fighting injustice.

397 • The old-school, tough-guy charm is one of Yul Brynner's exotic fortes.

*398* • Tony Curtis in a portrait from 1959, that highlights his soft manly looks.

*399* • Warren Beatty is still today considered one of the most fascinating actors of Hollywood's history.

Jean Paul Belmondo was consecrated as one of the most important French actors, in the minds of the audience and the critics alike, by the 1960 film *Breathless,* right, considered a manifesto of the Nouvelle Vague.

● Steve McQueen, left, on the set of *The Great Escape* (1963), is remembered not only for his undeniable acting talent, but also for his passion for motorcycle racing.

- Peter O'Toole, turbulent Irish actor, reached international fame with *Lawrence of Arabia*, a 1962 movie that won seven Oscars.

Alain Delon, here on the set of *The Last Adventure (1967)*, directed by Robert Enrico, embodies the male prototype of candid yet glacial beauty.

Robert Redford, as the outlaw Sundance Kid, and Paul Newman, as the bandit Butch Cassidy, in the 1969 western *Butch Cassidy*, directed by George Roy Hill and chosen for preservation in the National Film Registry of the United States Library of Congress in 2003.

When asked who he liked as an actor, Sergio Leone used to answer: "I like Clint Eastwood because he's an actor who only has two expressions: one with his hat on and one without his hat on." Eastwood (here in a picture from 1969), who became famous for his "tough-guy" roles, actually revealed himself an incredibly versatile actor, director, film producer and soundtrack composer.

○ Elegant, cold and seductive, Sean Connery is perfect for the role of James Bond (left). But he manages to avoid being completely identified with Ian Fleming's character and shows off his talent playing different complex roles like sheriff O'Niel in *Outland* (1981), right.

Regarded as one of world's best actors, Robert De Niro has often played fascinating yet emotionally unstable characters as in *Once Upon a Time in America* (1984), directed by Sergio Leone, (left), and in *The Deer Hunter* (1978) by Michael Cimino (right).

416 • Al Pacino plays the ruthless gangster Tony Montana with great intensity in *Scarface*, directed by Brian De Palma in 1983.

417 • In *The Devil's Advocate* (1997), Al Pacino displays his powerful theatricality.

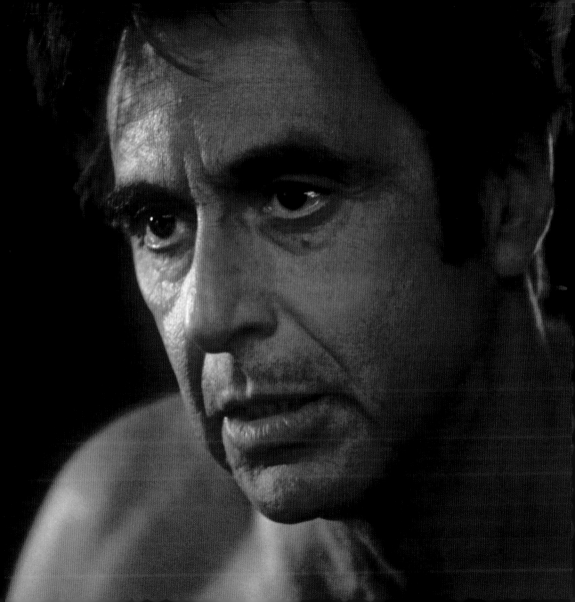

418 • Hugh Grant in a scene from *Notting Hill* (1999) a romantic comedy that was successful with both audiences and critics.

419 • A portrait of Michael Douglas, a man of great temperament who delighted the public thanks to the intensity of his gaze and his undisputed acting skills.

Harrison Ford in the role that gave him his worldwide success: the rugged space smuggler Han Solo in *Return of the Jedi* (1983) and the daring Professor Jones, archaeologist created by Steven Spielberg, in the second installment of the saga: *Indiana Jones and the Temple of Doom* (1984).

• John Travolta is still today the icon of the musicals of the 70s. Here he is on the left in a 1978 picture while playing Tony Manero in *Staying Alive* (1983).

*424* • Richard Gere in *Doctor T and the Women*, a 2000 film by Robert Altman, playing the part of a rich and esteemed gynecologist who will have to reconsider his whole life.

*425* • Richard Gere is a sex-symbol who has proved to have remarkable acting skills.

● Denzel Washington has proven to be an actor with an extraordinary versatility, as shown in *Power* (1986), left and *The Hurricane* (1999), right.

● Nick Nolte in a 1975 picture (left) and in the drama/action film *Who'll Stop The Rain* (right), in which he graces us with an intense performance.

Antonio Banderas in a scene from the film adaptation of the musical *Evita* (1996), and in *Desperado*, directed by Robert Rodriguez in 1995.

432 • Kurt Russell shows muscle and a real macho personality in *Big Trouble in Little China* (1986).

433 • A symbol of masculinity, in the 2003 action film *Tears of the Sun*, Bruce Willis is a commander that discovers his human side.

● Actor and director, Jack Nicholson made movie history with his unmistakable smile. He won three Oscars for *Someone Flew over the Cuckoo's Nest* (1975), *Terms of Endearment* (1983) and *As Good as It Gets* (1997). Right, a picture from the film.

436 • Sylvester Stallone is one of Hollywood's best muscle macho stars. This image is taken from *Lock Up* (1989).

437 • A former Mister Universe, Arnold Schwarzenegger has built himself a first-rate career as an action star. Here he is in *End of Days* (1999).

○ A male sex symbol from the very beginning, Brad Pitt forged ahead, making it big in Hollywood in 1991 with a part in Ridley Scott's *Thelma & Louise*. These two images are taken from another success of his: *Legends of The Fall* (1994).

440 • A young Brad Pitt starred with Robert Redford in the harrowing *A River Runs Through It* (1992).

441 • In *Seven years in Tibet* (1997) Pitt plays the explorer and mountaineer Heinrich Harrer.

442 • In *No way out* (1987), Kevin Costner is a marine officer wrongfully accused of murder and unwillingly involved in a dangerous power play.

443 • In 1988 in *Bull Durham,* Kevin Costner the actor plays a fading baseball player.

444 • Mel Gibson directs himself in the role of a rebel fighting against the English in *Braveheart* (1995), which takes place in 13th-century Scotland.

445 • *The Bounty* (1984), which made Mel Gibson famous, tells the story of the Royal Navy's most famous mutiny, which took place in the 18th century.

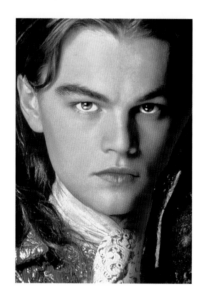

446 • In *The Iron Mask* (1999), Leonardo DiCaprio plays both Louis XIV and Philippe, the good twin, whom Louis imprisoned in the Bastille.

447 • In *The Beach* (1999), DiCaprio is a young American tourist searching for a natural paradise in Thailand, but who finds himself caught up in a dangerous situation.

● A more mature DiCaprio impersonates a diamond smuggler in *Blood Diamond* (2006), a film that takes place in Sierra Leone in 1999, during a bloody civil war.

*450* • In *A Few Good Men* (1992), Tom Cruise is a military lawyer working on a case.

*451* • Cruise is Captain Nathan Algren or "the last samurai," in the 2003 movie
of the same name.

452 • After the success of the first episode, Tom Cruise stars in *Mission Impossible* (2003).

453 • In 2001 Tom Cruise stars in *Vanilla Sky*, which also stars Penélope Cruz.

454 • In 2006 Daniel Craig, with his blonde hair and icy blue eyes, stars as James Bond, in the twenty-first episode of the series, *Casino Royale*.

455 • Pierce Brosnan was James Bond for four times and re-launched the character of Agent 007 after years of fiascos at the box-office

456 • In *L.A. Confidential* (1997) Russell Crowe plays the part of a cop in 1950s Los Angeles.

457 • The acting charisma of Russell Crowe was a success in the movie *The Gladiator* (2000) and helped him win an Oscar as best actor.

• Many-sided and versatile, Keanu Reeves was the ideal actor to be the lead role in the successful sci-fi trilogy of *The Matrix*.

*460-461* ● With rough looks and a dark stare, in 2004 Clive Owen is the main actor in *King Arthur*.

*461* ● Sweet and abrasive at the same time, Ewan McGregor stars in *Star Wars Episode III: Revenge of the Sith* (2005).

462 • Matt Damon, seen here acting in *Rounders* (1998), was very successful in *Will Hunting*.

462-463 • In 1997 the duo formed by Matt Damon and Ben Affleck conquers Hollywood by winning an Oscar for the screenplay of Good Will Hunting. From that moment the careers of the two friends go their own ways, allowing each to gain great success.

The sexy glamorous icon Jude Law stars in *Alfie* (2004), the story of a young English dandy in New York.

● In 1999 Jude Law obtained an Oscar nomination as best supporting actor for his role in the movie *The Talented Mr. Ripley*.

468 ● Orlando Bloom, with his intense, seductive stare, landed the role of Legolas, the elf in the fantasy trilogy of *The Lord of the Rings*.

469 ● Viggo Mortensen's face, with its intense expressive power, has made this actor one of the most appreciated in *The Lord of the Rings* saga.

● After the success of *The Lord of the Rings* Orlando Bloom works on another trilogy, *Pirates of the Caribbean*, where he plays the role of Will Turner.

472 • Johnny Depp at the 2001 Deauville American Film Festival.

473 • In the movie *Chocolat* (2000) Johnny Depp plays the charming gypsy leader, Roux.

● The gorgeous
and dark Johnny Depp
takes part in the 2007
Venice Film Festival to
hand the Golden Lion
to director Tim Burton.

476 • Will Smith as a narcotics cop in *Bad Boys II* (2003), the sequel to the same 1995 movie.

477 • Will Smith is the lonely protagonist of the sci-fi movie *I Am Legend* (2007).

Will Smith in a riveting scene from the movie *Bad Boys II* (2003).

*480* • George Clooney in *Ocean's Eleven* by Steven Soderberg (2001). The movie is a remake of the 1960 *Ocean's Eleven*.

*481* • George Clooney, 2007.

482 • Jake Gyllenhaal in *Proof* by John Madden, 2005.

483 • Matthew McConaughey in *Sahara* (2005).

# FRAMES
## of LOVE

Clark Gable embraces Vivien Leigh in *Gone With the Wind* (1939).

## INTRODUCTION Frames of Love

LOVE STORIES THAT BLOSSOMED IN FRONT OF THE CAMERA ARE COUNTLESS: WHETHER IT IS ORSON WELLES AND RITA HAYWORTH IN *THE LADY FROM SHANGHAI* (ORSON WELLES, 1947), ROGER VADIM AND BRIGITTE BARDOT IN *AND GOD CREATED WOMAN* (1956), OR TOM CRUISE AND NICOLE KIDMAN, WHO FELL IN LOVE ON THE SET OF *FAR AND AWAY* (RON HOWARD, 1992), AND WERE ABOUT TO SEPARATE IN THE MENTAL LABYRINTH OF *EYES WIDE SHUT* (STANLEY KUBRICK, 1999). IT IS ALMOST AS IF IN ADDITION TO HITTING THE HEARTS OF THE AUDIENCE, THE MAGIC OF THE LOVE SCENE HAS A DIS-RUPTIVE POWER OVER THE PRIVATE LIVES OF THE ACTORS AS WELL. SOME CONSIDER IT TO BE A GOLDEN RULE OF CINEMA, ALMOST A SEPARATE *MORAL CODE* (AND THEREFORE A CODE OF LOVE): AS IF CINEMA WERE A SACRED FESTIVITY – FALLING IN

## **INTRODUCTION** Frames of Love

LOVE INCLUDED – AND MOVIE STARS OFFICIATED ITS RITUALS. THIS IS PROBABLY WHY TODAY, MUCH LIKE IN A PROFANE PAN-THEON, BRAD PITT, THE GOD OF FIRE IGNITED ANGELINA JOLIE IN *MR. & MRS. SMITH* (DOUG LIMAN, 2005). BUT EVEN WHEN THE MOVIE DOES NOT HINT AT ANY TRUE BACKSTAGE LOVE, THE POWER OF EMOTION ENDS UP IMMORTALIZING SCENES AND STARS, BLENDING TRUTH AND FANTASY. THE DIVINE IN-STRUMENT THANKS TO WHICH THE SILVER SCREEN PROJECTS LOVE ONTO THE AUDIENCE IS NOT CUPID'S ARROW, BUT A KISS. HENCE WE HAVE VIGGO MORTENSEN IN *A HISTORY OF VIO-LENCE* (DAVID CRONENBERG, 2005) FURIOUSLY KISSING MARIA BELLO; AND BURT LANCASTER IN *FROM HERE TO ETERNITY* (FRED ZINNEMANN, 1953), PASSIONATELY KISSING THE LIPS OF DEBORAH KERR ON THE BEACH, IN ONE OF MOVIE HISTORY'S

# Frames of Love

Introduction

MOST FAMOUS SCENES; AND HARVEY KEITEL TRYING TO SE-DUCE AND THEN SHYLY KISSING THE UNREACHABLE HOLLY HUNTER IN *THE PIANO* (JANE CAMPION, 1993). ACROBATIC KISS-ES ARE ALWAYS A SUPERHERO'S DOMAIN AS PROVEN BY TO-BEY MAGUIRE AND THE ADORABLE KIRSTEN DUNST, IN THE SPI-DERMAN SAGA; WHEREAS KISSES THAT BECAME LEGENDARY, OR MOVIE ICONS, ARE WITHOUT A DOUBT THE ONES BETWEEN CLARK GABLE AND VIVIEN LEIGH IN VICTOR FLEMING'S *GONE WITH THE WIND* (1939). BUT THE MOST BEAUTIFUL AND THERE-FORE MOST MEMORABLE KISS IS THE ONE THAT NEVER HAP-PENED: OBVIOUSLY THE ONE BETWEEN HUMPHREY BOGART AND INGRID BERGMAN, ON THE AIRPORT RUNWAY IN *CASABLANCA* (1942).

● Kirsten Dunst kisses an acrobatic Tobey Maguire in *Spiderman* (2002).

● Clark Gable and Jean Harlow portrayed in two frames from the film *Hold Your Man* (1933): sprawled on a couch and in a passionate embrace.

*492* • Gregory Peck passionately kisses Audrey Hepburn in *Roman Holiday* (1953).

*493* • Katherine Hepburn smiles at James Stewart in *The Philadelphia Story* (1949).

*494-495* • John Wayne and Gail Russell in an affectionate exchange of glances
in *Angel and the Badman* (1947).

*496* ● The dome of the Capitol is a background for this sweet pose by Katharine Hepburn and Spencer Tracy in *State of the Union* (1948).

*497* ● Katharine Hepburn looks intensely at Spencer Tracy in *Woman of the Year* (1942).

*498-499* ● Lauren Bacall surrenders to Gary Cooper's arms in *Bright Leaf* (1950).

*500* • Kim Hunter seeks refuge in Marlon Brando's arms in *A Street Car Named Desire* (1951).

*501* • The lips of Tarita Teriipaia and Marlon Brando brush each other in *Mutiny on the Bounty* (1962).

*502-503* • One of the most famous love scenes of the history of cinema: Burt Lancaster kisses Deborah Kerr in *From Here to Eternity* (1953).

*504-505 and 506* • Two unforgettable frames from *To Catch A Thief* (1955): Grace Kelly drives a Spider next to Gary Cooper; the two due protagonists exchange sweet tenderness.

*507* • Elizabeth Taylor softly kisses Richard Burton in *The Taming of the Shrew* (1967).

*508-509* • Marilyn Monroe yields to Clark Gable in *The Misfits* (1961).

510 • Andie MacDowell kisses Hugh Grant under the rain in a moment of the comedy *Four Weddings and a Funeral* (1994).

511 • Once again the rain falling on two lovers: George Peppard and Audrey Hepburn, in *Breakfast at Tiffany's* (1961).

512 • Cary Grant and Ingrid Bergman's lips gently touch in *Notorious* (1946).

513 • An unforgettable cinema kiss: Anita Ekberg yields to Marcello Mastroianni in the Trevi fountain in *La dolce vita* (1960).

*514* ● Sean Connery passionately holds Honor Blackman in *Goldfinger* (1964).

*515* ● In this poster embrace Pierce Brosnan holds Izabella Scorupco tightly:
it is a promo for *Goldeneye* (1995).

● Robert Redford playing with Meryl Streep in a famous romantic scene from the movie *Out of Africa* (1985).

518 • All the happiness that comes from falling in love transpires from this frame from *One Fine Day* (1996), with actors George Clooney and Michelle Pfeiffer.

519 • Richard Gere softly kisses Debra Winger in *An Officer and a Gentleman* (1982).

520 • An embrace before leaving for the front: Lisa Eichhorn presses against Richard Gere in *Yanks* (1979).

521 • Tom Cruise smiles while relaxing with Elisabeth Shue, in a Caribbean scene from *Cocktail* (1988).

522 • Kathleen Turner and Michael Douglas kiss passionately in *The Jewel of the Nile* (1985).

523 • The gothic love of *Dracula* (1992) finds its place in the dark expressions of Winona Ryder and Gary Oldman.

● Love can be sad: Kim Basinger leans on Russell Crowe's shoulder in *L.A. Confidential* (1997).

● Kevin Costner takes Robin Wright Penn in his arms on the "boat of destiny" in *Message in a Bottle* (1999).

528 • A kiss between Leonardo DiCaprio and Kate Winslet is the image and icon of the dramatic blockbuster *Titanic* (1997).

529 • A particularly sensual Penélope Cruz holds Tom Cruise's face in *Vanilla Sky* (2001).

530 ● Leonardo DiCaprio and Cameron Diaz loving each other in the dramatic and violent *Gangs of New York* (2002).

531 ● When love is lost in space: the lips of Harrison Ford gently press against those of Carrie Fisher in *The Empire Strikes Back* (1980).

532 • Demi Moore and Patrick Swayze have one last night of love in *Ghost* (1990).

533 • Tenderness and passion in this kiss between Sienna Miller and Heath Ledger, in a frame from *Casanova* (2005).

● Keira Knightley and Michael Pitt lose themselves in each other's arms in the springtime of *Silk* (2007).

536 • The hottest love scene in movie history is probably the one between Jessica Lange and Jack Nicholson in *The Postman Always Rings Twice* (1981).

537 • The happiness of holding each other once again: as expressed by Penélope Cruz and Matthew McConaughey in *Sahara* (2005).

538 • An unconventional kiss between superheroes: Michelle Pfeiffer "tastes" Michael Keaton's lips in *Batman Returns* (1992).

539 • Kate Bosworth tenderly looks at Brandon Routh in *Superman Returns* (2006).

● The most "tangled" kiss of movie history is the one between Tobey Maguire and Kirsten Dunst in *Spiderman 3* (2007).

# BABY STARS

- *Stand Up and Cheer*, in American theatres in 1934, brings fame to Shirley Temple, who will become the most famous *enfant-prodige* of 1930s America.

## INTRODUCTION Baby Stars

CHILD STARS OR STARS AS CHILDREN? THE QUESTION BEGS FOR A CONSIDERATION: SHOULD WE FOCUS OUR ATTENTION ON THOSE ACTORS WHO FOUND SUCCESS PLAYING CHILD ROLES AND NEVER MANAGED TO DEPART FROM THAT CLICHÉ, OR ON THE MORE OR LESS FORTUNATE CHILDHOOD, CINEMATOGRAPHICALLY SPEAKING, OF THE MOST SUCCESSFUL MOVIE STARS? THE FIRST ROLES PLAYED BY GEORGE CLOONEY AND JULIA ROBERTS, OR THE LONG BRIGHT STREAK OF SHIRLEY TEMPLE'S SUCCESSFUL FILMS? CINEMA HISTORY IS RICH WITH CHILD ACTORS. SOME WERE METEORS, OTHER GREW BUT HAD TO DRASTICALLY CHANGE BECAUSE OF THE UNFORGIVING CAMERA. NOT ALL CHILDREN IN THE MOVIES ARE LIKE GIORGIO CANTARINI, THE

Macaulay Culkin becomes Hollywood's most famous diminutive star in 1991 with the movie *Home Alone*, which he follows with *My Girl*.

## **INTRODUCTION** Baby Stars

YOUNG SUPPORTING ACTOR IN ROBERTO BENIGNI'S LIFE IS
BEAUTIFUL (1997); NOT EVERYONE OBTAINED THE SUCCESS
THAT BEFELL NATALIE PORTMAN, WHO WAS BUT A CHILD IN
LUC BESSON'S LEON (1994). SOME HAD UNRECOGNIZABLE
DEBUTS. DOWNWARD STARE AND CHUBBY CHEEKS: THIS IS
MARLENE DIETRICH, WHO WAS A LITTLE GIRL IN THE MOVIES
OF THE WEIMAR ERA (1923-1925), WHEN STERNBERG
HADN'T YET ARRIVED IN BERLIN, IN 1930, TO FILM THE BLUE
ANGEL AND TO RAISE HER CHEEKS, EMACIATE HER FACE
AND SHARPEN HER STARE. THE CHUBBY GIRL THUS UNNA-
TURALLY BECAME THE DIVA WE ALL REMEMBER. AND WHAT
ABOUT INGRID BERGMAN? GUSTAV MOLANDER DISCOVE-
RED HER AS AN UNSOPHISTICATED TEENAGER: INTERMEZZO
(1936) SHOWED A VERY YOUNG BERGMAN WHO LACKED

## INTRODUCTION Baby Stars

THE MALICE SHE POSSESSES IN DOCTOR JEKYLL AND MISTER HIDE (VICTOR FLEMING, 1941), WHO LACKED THAT CERTAIN CHARM, INSECURITY, PASSION AND CONTRAST WE THOUGHT WAS NATURALLY HERS. THE PROTOTYPE OF THE CHILD STAR OF MODERN CINEMA IS DREW BARRYMORE, THE CUTE CHILD PROTAGONIST OF E.T. THE EXTRA-TERRESTRIAL (STEVEN SPIELBERG, 1982). SHE OBTAINED A BOATLOAD OF SUCCESS, BUT ALSO HAD A DIFFICULT ADOLESCENCE AND A STRENUOUS RETURN TO NORMAL LIFE AND TO THE WORLD OF CINEMA. LITTLE GIRLS, BESIDES BEING FERTILE GROUND FOR THE WORLD OF CINEMA, AS PROVEN BY LUCHINO VISCONTI'S BELLISSIMA (1951), ARE EXCEPTIONAL MONEY MACHINES. BEAR IN MIND THAT THE NOW GLOBAL PHENOMENON OF MERCHANDISING WAS

# Baby Stars

Introduction

BORN IN 1934 WITH THE DEAL BETWEEN FOX AND IDEAL TOY TO DISTRIBUTE A DOLL THAT REPRESENTS THE BELOVED MINI-STAR SHIRLEY TEMPLE, THE LITTLE GIRL FROM CURLY TOP (IRVING CUMMINGS, 1935). HER CONTRACT QUICKLY BROUGHT HER MOTHER $70,000, AN INCREDIBLE AMOUNT OF MONEY FOR THAT TIME. FOR MONEY, SHIRLEY TEMPLE HAD TO REMAIN A LITTLE GIRL FOREVER. THE SAME MECHANISM, IN PROPORTION, HAPPENED TO BROOKE SHIELDS, JODIE FOSTER, MACAULAY CULKIN; OF THESE, ONLY FOSTER MANAGED TO ESCAPE THE WORKINGS OF ETERNAL CHILDHOOD AND TO BUILD HERSELF A PRESENT-DAY CAREER AS A MATURE ACTRESS.

- Only seven years old Drew Barrymore plays Gertie, the little sister of Elliot, the young man who befriends the cute alien in *E.T. the Extra-Terrestrial* by Steven Spielberg, filmed in 1982.

*550 and 551* • In *The Kid* (1921), Charlie Chaplin takes care of little Jackie Coogan.

*552-553* • Shirley Temple acts with Lionel Barrymore in *The Little Colonel* (1935).

554 • Shirley Temple, aka "dimples," greets her admirers from a car in 1936, when the extraordinary success of her movies had already made her a small diva.

555 • On 14 March 1935 the little wonder girl is consecrated as a international star as she writes her name in cement at the Grauman's Chinese Theatre on Hollywood Boulevard.

*556* • Mickey Rooney jokes around with Judy Garland in *Love Finds Andy Hardy*, 1938.

*556-557* • Already in 1932, Mickey Rooney had starred with Tom Brown and Maureen O'Sullivan in *Fast Companions*.

558 • *Strike Up the Band* (1940), stars Mickey Rooney with his friend Judy Garland.

559 • Young Judy Garland, here in *Love Finds Andy Hardy*, 1938, the child of showbiz parents, is just a little girl when she hits provincial theatres with her two older sisters.

• In the Clarence Brown movie *National Velvet* (1944), Elizabeth Taylor is triumphant with her character Velvet Brown, a young girl who passionately trains her horse to take part in the Grand National.

562 • A young Ron Howard, future famed director, plays the role of Glenn Ford's son in *The Courtship of Eddie's Father* by Vincente Minnelli, 1963.

563 • In 1962 Ron Howard played a funny budding musician in *The Music Man* by Morton Da Costa.

● Matthew Garber and Karen Dotrice are the siblings in *Mary Poppins* (1964), with Julie Andrews. The little actors wander on the roofs together with Dick Van Dyke the chimney-sweeper.

566 ● A bold Tatum O'Neal stands up to grumpy Walter Matthau, the drunken coach in *The Bad News Bears* (1976), a movie about a little-league baseball team.

567 ● Tatum O'Neal was very successful with her father Ryan in *Paper Moon* (1973).

- Jodie Foster, future Oscar winner, is one of the young characters in *Tom Sawyer* (1973): her first experience in acting dates back to the previous year, when she worked in *Napoleon and Samantha*.

In 1979 Ricky Schroeder works with Jon Voight in *The Champ*, directed by Franco Zeffirelli, which tells the moving tale of a former boxing champion and his son.

In 1978 a provocative Brooke Shields created a scandal playing the role of a prostitute in *Pretty Baby*, by Louis Malle, alongside Keith Carradine. The movie takes place in a beginning-of-the-century New Orleans and tells the story of lost innocence and love between the young prostitute and the French photographer who marries her.

574 • Corey Feldman, Ke Huy Quan, Kerri Green and Martha Plimpton are the cast of *The Goonies* (1985), a cult movie for kids of the 80s, which tells the tale of a gang of rambunctious young adventurers caught up in fantastic escapades, among pirates ships and hidden treasures.

575 • Sean Astin, between Ke Huy Quan and Corey Feldman, is the main character in *The Goonies*.

576 • Natalie Portman is the extraordinary Mathilda in *Léon (The Professional)*, directed by Luc Besson in 1994.

577 • Winona Ryder is a creepy teen in *Beetlejuice* (1988).

578 ● Macaulay Culkin's great expressiveness in *Home Alone 2: Lost in New York* (1992) renews the success of the movie that made him famous.

579 ● Macaulay takes on an unorthodox pastime in the first movie of the series.

An extremely young Leonardo DiCaprio acts in *What's Eating Gilbert Grape* (1993), a drama directed by Lasse Hallström in which he plays the role of the mentally challenged younger brother of the main character Gilbert (Johnny Depp): a moving story about a difficult family situation in the suffocating environment of American suburbia.

Another child prodigy of American cinema is Christina Ricci, who plays the little pest Wednesday in *The Addams Family* (1991), who came back in front of the camera two years later in the sequel *The Addams Family Values* (right).

● Kirsten Dunst as Amy March at a young age in *Little Women* (1994). In the same year, Dunst had successfully played the less reassuring character of a little vampire-girl in *Interview with the Vampire*.

● In *Star Wars - Episode I - The Phantom Menace* (1999), Jake Lloyd plays the role of little Anakin Skywalker, a kind and unselfish nine-year-old slave, who in reality is the Chosen One.

*588* • Abigail Breslin, only 10 years old, receives an *Oscar* nomination as best supporting actress for her role as Olive, a little American suburban beauty queen in *Little Miss Sunshine* (2006).

*589* • Cute Jonathan Lipnicki stars as little Ray in *Jerry Maguire* (1996).

590 • Jamie Bell shows all his unstoppable energy as the lead in *Billy Elliot* (2000).

591 • A very young Scarlett Johansson acts as the fourteen-year-old Grace MacLean in *The Horse Whisperer* (1998)s, directed by Robert Redford. .

592 • Daniel Radcliffe (Harry), Rupert Grint (Ron) and Emma Watson (Hermione), here in *Harry Potter and the Philosopher's Stone* (2001), the first movie of the series, are the three most famous faces of the saga.

593 • Daniel Radcliffe grew with his character: here he is in 2001.

● Dakota Fanning (left) is little Rachel in *War of the Worlds*, (2005), a sci-fi film by Steven Spielberg. From the same director is the futuristic *Artificial Intelligence: A.I.* (2001), which stars Haley Joel Osment (right).

596 • In *Finding Neverland* (2004), with Johnny Depp, little Freddie Highmore plays the part of Peter Llewellyn Davies, the child who would inspire Scottish writer James Matthew Barrie to create the character of Peter Pan.

597 • Freddie Highmore with the Psammead in *Five Children and It* (2004).

# BEYOND the CAMERA

Marilyn Monroe shows off some acrobatics on the beach in the 50s.

# INTRODUCTION Beyond the Camera

The GREAT DEPRESSION ERA THAT BEGAN 1929 PARADOXICALLY COINCIDES WITH HOLLY-WOOD'S GOLDEN AGE, AS IF THE DREAMS AND WISHES OF ALL THE AUDIENCE, FRUSTRATED BY RE-ALITY, WERE TO FIND THEIR REDEMPTION ON THE SILVER SCREEN. IN THOSE DAYS A TIMID CURIOSITY, THAT TODAY IS PERVASIVE, STARTED TO TAKE SHAPE: KNOWING ABOUT CELEBRITY LIFE, TO BE USED AS A COUNTERPOINT TO NORMAL LIFE AND MAYBE TO SEE ITS DEVIANCY. IN THOSE DAYS, THE UNSCRUPULOUS PRIVATE LIFE OF A CELEBRITY WAS CONSIDERED A TERRIBLE EXAMPLE AND, ABOVE ALL, IT WAS A HARBINGER OF WANING EARNINGS.

• Shirley MacLaine sips tea with her daughter Sachi Parker, 1959.

## INTRODUCTION Beyond the Camera

THE FIRST "HISTORICAL" SCANDAL WAS THE SUICIDE OF OLIVE THOMAS, THE WIFE OF JACK PICKFORD AND THE STAR OF SELZNICK PICTURES, A MOTION PICTURE STUDIO WHOSE MOTTO WAS "MAKING MOVIES TO MAKE HAPPY FAMILIES." FROM THAT EPISODE ON, THE DETRACTORS OF HOLLYWOOD ACCUSED STARS SUCH AS CHARLIE CHAPLIN, MARY PICKFORD, DOUGLAS FAIRBANKS, RODOLFO VALENTINO, GLORIA SWANSON AND GRETA GARBO OF LEADING IMMORAL LIVES. IN 1934 THE HAYS CODE DECIDED TO TAKE CORRECTIVE ACTION. FOR PRIVATE LIFE AND FILMS, A COMMON MORAL GROUND WAS OBLIGATORY: MARRIAGE AND FAMILY WERE ACCEPTABLE WHEREAS ADULTERY AND SEX WERE PROHIBITED: IT WAS A

## INTRODUCTION Beyond the Camera

STRONG BAN ON IMMORALITY AND DEBAUCHERY UNLESS EVIL WERE PUT ON FILM, ONLY TO BE BEATEN BY GOOD. FROM THAT MOMENT ON, IMAGES OF IDYLLIC AND "NORMAL" LIFE BEGAN TO CIRCULATE: FEMALE STARS BATHING AT THE BEACH OR IN THE POOL, MALE STARS PLAYING WITH THEIR KIDS, A COUPLE OF STARS ON VACATION OR WALKING THEIR DOG. STARS WERE "DISCIPLINED" FROM ABOVE, FROM FRED ASTAIRE TO BETTE DAVIS, TO THE METHOD ACTORS OF THE ACTORS STUDIO, FROM MONTGOMERY CLIFT TO MARLON BRANDO. MANY TRIED TO BELIEVE IN IT, STAGING ROMANTIC ACTS OF DAILY LIFE: A GOOD EXAMPLE OF THIS ARE SOME "FAMILY" PICTURES THAT PORTRAY BURT LANCASTER

# Beyond the Camera
## Introduction

WITH HIS WIFE AND FOUR CHILDREN, OR JOHN WAYNE READING THE PAPER TO HIS NUMEROUS CHILDREN, OR INGRID BERGMAN AT THE WINDOW OF A TRAIN CAR WITH THE CHILDREN SHE HAD BY ROSSELLINI. THE MOST RECENT STORY, DUE ALSO TO THE GROWING NUMBER OF MEDIA AND THE UBIQUITY OF COMMUNICATION MEANS, BROKE THIS FRAGILE YET HYPOCRITICAL BARRIER: TODAY THE PRIVATE LIFE OF THE STARS IS OFFERED ALMOST AS A COROLLARY OF LIFE ON THE SCREEN, SOMETIMES, IN EXTREME CASES, BECOMING A MEANS OF MARKETING AND A SELLABLE PRODUCT.

- Paul Newman and his wife Joanne Woodward joking after immortalizing their handprints in the cement of the *Walk of Fame*.

● Carole Lombard and Clark Gable in two moments of fun in their California ranch, 1939.

*608* • Rita Hayworth playing by the pool with daughter Rebecca and husband Orson Welles, 1944.

*609* • Rita Hayworth having fun in the pool with an inflatable horsey, 1940.

*610* ● Hollywood child prodigies having fun at a party.

*611* ● A very young Judy Garland plays with Mickey Rooney and Jackie Cooper during her sixteenth birthday party.

*612* • Burt Lancaster shows his daughter the secrets of a film set.

*613* • Bette Davis proudly watches her daughter.

614 • Kirk Douglas pictured here while playing with his son Michael.

615 • John Wayne in the unusual role of family man while reading a magazine.

616-617 • This sequence portrays Marilyn Monroe while intent on gardening, 1960.

C 8668

C 8671

CB677

CB676

● Marilyn Monroe absorbed by thoughts and words on her home couch, 1943.

618

• Marilyn Monroe with her second husband, the playwright Arthur Miller, 1962.

*622* • Humphrey Bogart and Lauren Bacall read a script together, 1944.

*623* • Lauren Bacall and Humphrey Bogart engaged in a conversation in front of their home hearth, 1944.

624 • Lauren Bacall and Humphrey Bogart chatting outside the studio dressing room, 1945.

625 • Lauren Bacall and Humphrey Bogart enjoying their sailboat in the 40s.

626 ● Gregory Peck smiles for the camera holding his son's hand, 1945.

627 ● Gregory Peck plays with his sons and wife Greta, 1946.

628 • Michael Wilding and Elizabeth Taylor in the park with little Michael Howard, 1953.

629 • Elizabeth Taylor laughs while "assaulted" by the pigeons in Trafalgar Square, London, 1948.

630 ● It's 1942 and Mickey Rooney and Ava Gardner, newly married, have fun playing the piano in the suite of the Ritz Carlton in Boston.

631 ● Brigitte Bardot and Roger Vadim in their Paris house, 1952.

During production pauses of *Listen, Darling* (1938), Judy Garland has fun playing baseball and relaxes in her dressing room.

Frank Sinatra and Ava Gardner sitting at a private table sipping a drink, 1951. Sinatra is Gardner's third husband, while Gardner is the second wife of Sinatra.

A romantic seaside walk, Frank Sinatra and Ava Gardner, Miami, 1951.

*638* • Rita Hayworth in a rare scene of domestic life, is busy making sweets, 1950.

*639* • Rita Hayworth in the car with her daughters Yasmine, in the nanny's arms, and Rebecca, from her wedding with Orson Welles, 1951.

*640-641* • Burt Lancaster sitting at the table with his children and his second wife Norma, 1954.

● Ingrid Bergman and
Roberto Rossellini
looking over the Grand
Canal Grande from the
balcony of a Venetian
hotel, 1950.

644 • Ingrid Bergman enjoys some fresh air with her son Roberto and the twins Isabella and Ingrid, 1958.

645 • From a departing train, Ingrid Bergman and her three children bid the city of Rome farewell, 1955.

646 • Audrey Hepburn smiles at her husband Mel Ferrer while he holds her with a warm embrace, 1956.

647 • Audrey Hepburn and Mel Ferrer in formal attire on the day of their wedding, 25 September 1954.

648 • In the Switzerland of the early 50s, Audrey Hepburn on board a motorboat, wearing a funny small hat.

649 • Audrey Hepburn suggests a swing in an improbable golf uniform, 1955.

● Two enchanting smiles from Katharine Hepburn in the 50s.

*652* • Tony Curtis with his wife Janet Leigh and daughter Kelly Lee.

*653* • Brand new parents Tony Curtis and Janet Leigh watching their daughter Kelly Lee.

654 • Romy Schneider kisses her boyfriend Alain Delon, who has just been given an award at the Musical Festival in Torvaianica, 1961.

655 • Romy Schneider has a ball while Alain Delon holds her on his shoulders, 1958.

*656* • Paul Newman and Joanne Woodward posing with a knowing smile.

*657* • The deep understanding between Paul Newman and Joanne Woodward transpires even in this intense glance, 1961.

Judy Garland spending some free time with her husband, Vincente Minnelli, and her daughter little Liza, a future Hollywood star.

660 • Julie Andrews is busy feeding her little Emma Kate, 1964.

661 • A warm affectionate exchange between mother and daughter, Julie Andrews and Emma Kate, 1965.

# COSMETICS and MAKE-UP

- The features of Peter Sellers, the witty and eclectic English actor are transformed by make-up in *The Fiendish Plot of Dr. Fu Manchu* (1980).

## INTRODUCTION Cosmetics and Make-Up

Is MAKE-UP SOMETHING ARTIFICIAL (BE IT SIMPLE MAKE-UP OR PROSTHESES OR AN ELABORATE COSTUME) THAT *IS APPLIED* TO A MOVIE STAR RIGHT BEFORE "CAMERAS, ACTION!" (A PRACTICE THAT FINDS ITS ROOTS IN THE HISTORY OF THEATER), OR IS IT SOMETHING THAT PARADOXICALLY *IS REMOVED*? THE ANSWER NATURALLY IS: BOTH. IF IT IS TRUE THAT GREASEPAINT, MASCARA AND WIGS ARE ALSO IN PRESENT-DAY MOVIES, IT IS INTERESTING TO SEE HOW DURING THE DECADES THE BEST MAKE-UP TECHNIQUES HAVE ENDED UP BLURRING WITH SPECIAL EFFECTS, COMPLETELY HIDING THE

In *Batman and Robin* (1997), Uma Thurman and Arnold Schwarzenegger wear the garish costumes of Poison Ivy and Mr. Freeze, the superhero's antagonists.

## INTRODUCTION Cosmetics and Make-Up

ACTOR'S BODY. THAT TOO IS MAKE-UP. IT IS PROBA-
BLY THE LINE THAT DEFINES THE DIFFERENCE BE-
TWEEN MODERN MAKE-UP AND PRE-CONTEMPO-
RARY MAKE-UP: WHICH IMPLIES SOMETHING THAT
IS *ADDED* TO THE BODY OF THE MOVIE STAR, FROM
LON CHANEY'S FANGS IN *THE PHANTOM OF THE
OPERA* (GASTON LEROUX, 1925), TO JERRY LEWIS'
GROTESQUE DENTURE IN *THE NUTTY PROFESSOR*
(1963). BUT LET'S NOT MAKE THIS A MATTER OF
PAST AND PRESENT; IN REALITY EVEN TODAY'S CIN-
EMA RESERVES THE MAKE-UP ARTIST A PRIMARY
ROLE: WHAT WOULD JIM CARREY HAVE BEEN WITH-
OUT THE MULTIPLE MASKS PAINTED ON HIS FACE IN
BRAD SIBERLING'S *LEMONY SNICKET* (2004)? AND

## INTRODUCTION Cosmetics and Make-Up

HOW WOULD DUSTIN HOFFMAN HAVE BEEN CREDI-
BLE IN THE DIFFICULT YET AMUSING FEMALE ROLE
OF *TOOTSIE* (SIDNEY POLLACK, 1982)? THESE ARE
THE "CAKED-ON MASKS" FROM A TYPE OF CINEMA
THAT TODAY CAN BE CALLED SLIGHTLY DATED, YET
NOT OUTDATED. AND IF THE AGED ORSON WELLES
IN *CITIZEN KANE* (1941) STILL REPRESENTS A MODEL
FOR ALL MAKE-UP ARTISTS, DAVID PROWSE WITH
OR WITHOUT HIS DARTH VADER HELMET IN *THE EM-
PIRE STRIKES BACK* (GEORGE LUCAS, 1981) OR A
WELL MADE-UP JOHNNY DEPP IN GORE VERBINS-
KI'S *PIRATES OF THE CARIBBEAN - DEAD MAN'S
CHEST* (2006), PROVE THAT TRADITIONAL MAKE-UP
STILL HAS A PLACE BEHIND THE SCENES OF FILM

# Cosmetics and Make-Up

## Introduction

PRODUCTION. WILL IT ALWAYS BE THAT WAY? DEFINITELY NOT: CONTEMPORARY CINEMA IS REPLACING BRUSH AND SPATULA WITH MOUSE AND KEYBOARD. HENCE WE GO BACK TO OUR INITIAL CONSIDERATION: COVERING MAKE-UP WILL BE REPLACED BY REVEALING MAKE-UP AND NO ONE WILL MISS GREASEPAINT. A PERFECT EXAMPLE COMES ONCE AGAIN FROM *PIRATES OF THE CARIBBEAN*: DAVY JONES, CAPTAIN SPARROW'S ANTAGONIST HAS A SQUID HEAD AND A TENTACLE BEARD. DIGITAL BEAUTY OBVIOUSLY NEEDS NO MAKE-UP.

- In the beginning of their career Jim Carey and Jeff Goldblum were the funny furry red and blue aliens in the comedy *Earth Girls Are Easy* (1988).

● In 1940, the extraordinary comedy couple formed by Stan Laurel and Oliver Hardy, stars in *A Chump at Oxford,* a movie that became famous for the funny portrayal of a curly blonde waitress by Laurel.

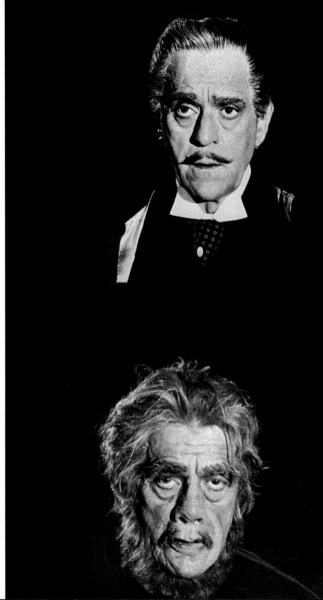

○ This sequence shows the work of make-up artists that transformed Boris Karloff from Doctor Jekyll to Mr. Hyde in *Abbott and Costello Meet Dr. Jekyll and Mr. Hyde* (1953).

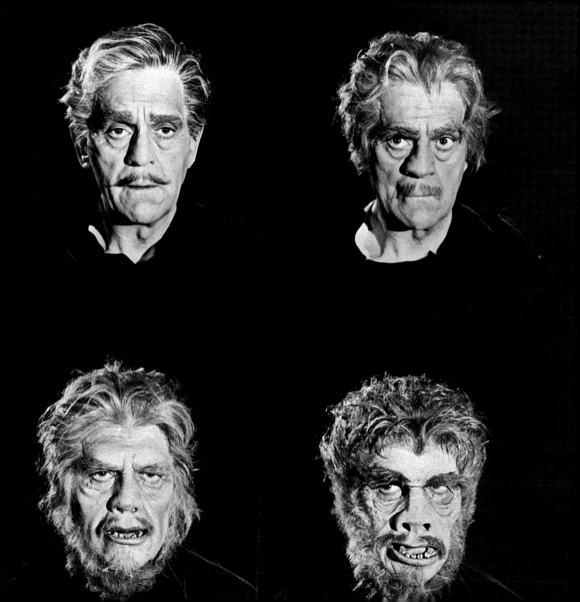

● To play the role of the monster in *Frankenstein* (1931), Boris Karloff is forced to sit through grueling make-up sessions, over six hours long.

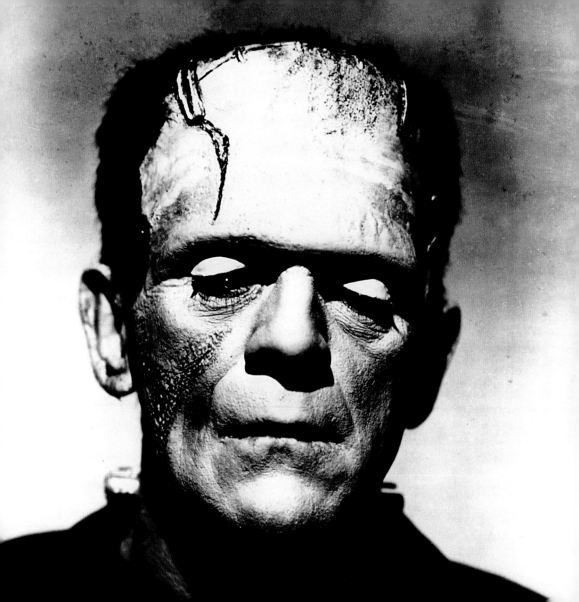

● On the set of the movie *The Teahouse of the August Moon* Glenn Ford looks on, surprised and amused, as Marlon Brando is busy personally attending to his transformation into the Japanese character Sakini.

• The heavy make-up needed to transform Jack Lemmon and Tony Curtis into Josephine and Daphne in *Some Like It Hot* (1959), created two movie history icons.

● In *My Geisha* (1962), the transformation of Shirley MacLaine into a Japanese geisha, obtained with make-up, is the element around which the whole comedy unfolds.

● The exceptional qualities of Peter Sellers enable him to play three roles: in *Dr. Strangelove*, (1964) (left), in *The Mouse That Roared* (1959) (right), where he even plays an old duchess.

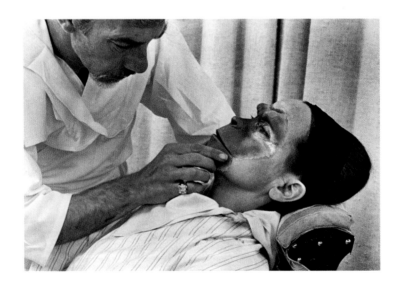

• The visual impact of the make-up in *Planet of the Apes* (1968) was such that in the Academy Awards the make-up received a special Oscar.

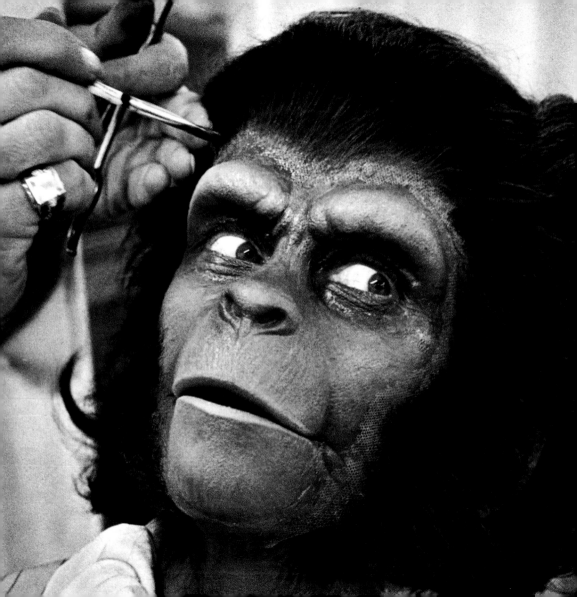

● Peter Sellers' transformational skills in *The Fiendish Plot of Dr. Fu Manchu* (1980), are aided by a very effective make-up.

● Once again make-up has a central role: in 1982 it helps Dustin Hoffman play a female role in the comedy *Tootsie*.

● In *Terminator* (1984), make-up transforms Arnold Schwarzenegger into a frightful cyborg and makes the illusion ever more credible.

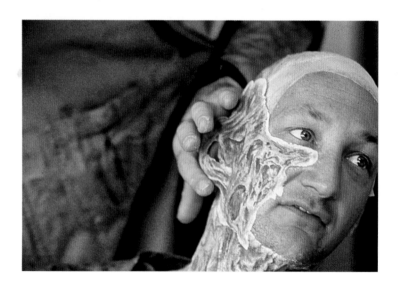

- Often in horror movies the work of make-up artists becomes a fundamental instrument in creating suggestion: who would be afraid of Freddy Krüger from *Nightmare on Elm Street* without the ravaging scars covering his whole body?

In the movies taken from the Batman comics, the looks of the "bad guys" are made grotesque by extreme make-up, such as in the case of Jack Nicholson's Joker and Danny DeVito's deformed Penguin.

In 1988 the Oscar for best make-up was awarded to *Beetlejuice* for the cadaveric make-up on Winona Ryder and Michael Keaton, who played the cheeky demon.

An unrecognizable
Dustin Hoffman plays
Captain Hook in *Hook*,
the 1991 film directed
by Steven Spielberg.

• The incredible expressive skills of Johnny Depp are sometimes highlighted by extreme make-up: as in *Edward Scissorhands* (1990), left, and *Sweeney Todd: The Demon Barber of Fleet Street* (2007).

● In 1992 Gary Oldman is the lead in *Bram Stoker's Dracula*, a film that deservedly won an Oscar for best make-up.

In the comedy *Mrs. Doubtfire* (1993), we follow the transformation of the explosive Robin Williams into an old housekeeper thanks to make-up.

It is very difficult to recognize actor Patrick Swayze under the make-up and the flashy clothes of the drag queen Vida Bohemme, in the 1995 comedy *To Wong Foo, Thanks for Everything! Julie Newmar*.

● Whether he is wearing the angry mask of the Grinch in the homonymous 2000 film, left, or the exuberant one in *The Mask* (1994), right, Jim Carrey's facial expressions do not go unnoticed.

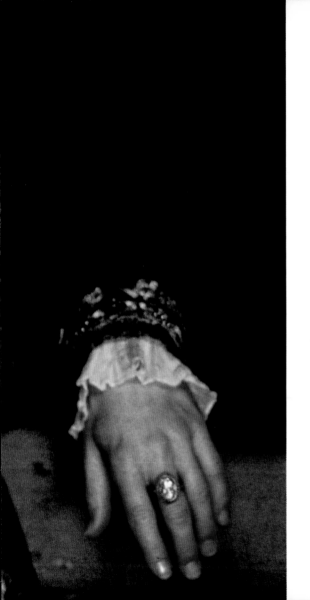

*710-7111* • In 1994 Tom Cruise abandons the role of the American hero to star in the horror drama *Interview with the Vampire*.

*711* • An unrecognizable John Travolta made up as an alien in *Battlefield Earth* (2000).

• In *Mary Shelley's Frankenstein* (1994).Robert De Niro gives life to a monster with human expressions and feelings, aided by a make-up that leaves the stereotypes from the past behind to create a face disfigured by scars, yet definitely more expressive.

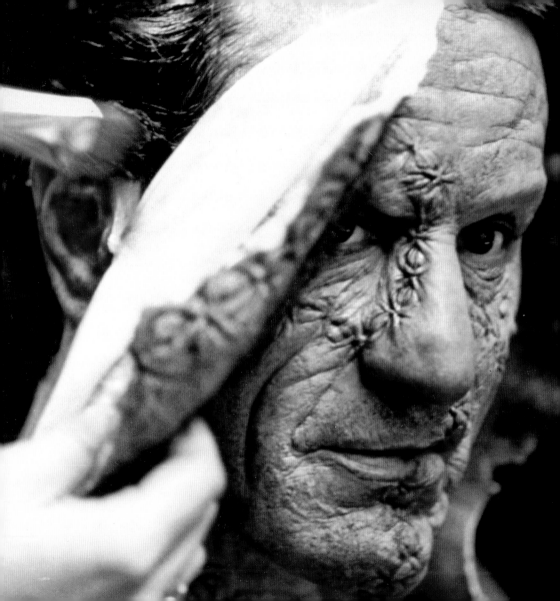

- In *Norbit* (2007), a chameleonic changeling Eddie Murphy, thanks to an extreme use of make-up, can convincingly play all the main roles in the movie.

● The power of make-up: even the gorgeous Monica Bellucci, left, and Sigourney Weaver, right, become horrible witches in *The Brothers Grimm* (2005) and *Snow White: A Tale of Terror* (1997).

When make-up and digital effects meet, it is possible to hide Bill Nighy's features under the tentacles of the squid-man in *Dead Man's Chest* (2006).

● Three hours of make-up were necessary to transform Jim Carrey into the evil Count Olaf in the movie *Lemony Snicket's A Series of Unfortunate Events* (2004).

The fans hoping for John Travolta's return to the musical did not expect to see him in the musical *Hairspray* (2007), as Edna. The incredible transformation was created through hours of make-up, facial prostheses and gel-padded costumes.

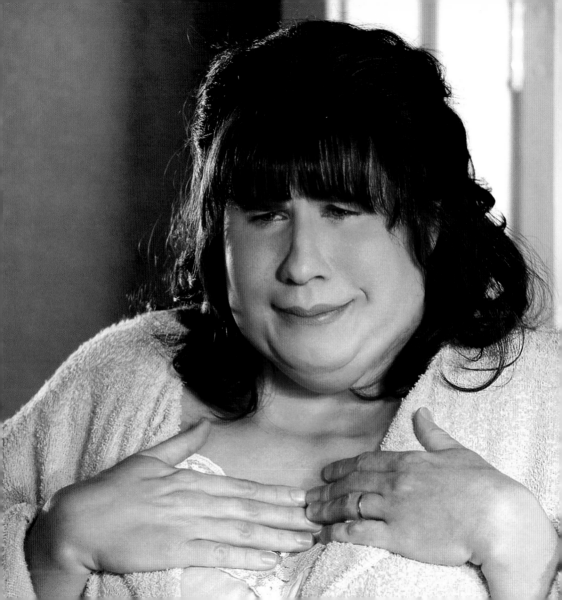

*724 and 725* ● Cate Blanchett accepted and won a tough challenge: to play the part of Bob Dylan in the documentary *I'm Not There* (2007).

*726-727* ● Eddie Murphy doubles up to play two of the main roles in *Norbit* (2007).

# AUTHOR Biographies

# INDEX

## VALERIA MANFERTO DE FABIANIS

She is the editor of the series. Valeria Manferto De Fabianis was born in Vercelli, Italy and studied arts at the Università Cattolica del Sacro Cuore in Milan, graduating with a degree in philosophy.

She is an enthusiastic traveler and nature lover. She has collaborated on the production of television documentaries and articles for the most prestigious Italian specialty magazines and has also written many photography books.

She co-founded Edizioni White Star in 1984 with Marcello Bertinetti and is the editorial director.

## GABRIELE BARRERA

Gabriele Barrera, who was born in Turin, is a professor of Film Theory and Production at Turin Polytechnic. He is a member of the Italian association of journalists and of SNCCI (Sindacato Nazionale Critici Cinematografici Italiani) and FIPRESCI (Fédération Internationale de la Presse Cinématographique) and is a newspaper journalist and contributor to Italian magazines including *Nick FilmTV, Duellanti, Donna, Cinecritica,* and *Maxim* and to English magazines including *Senses of Cinema,* and *Film Program.* Barrera is a member of the International Federation of Film Critics and has been a juror at international film festivals in Berlin, Venice, and Locarno. He is an author of many volumes about film, among which are *Da Umberto D a Europa 51, L'eccesso della visione, La bella è la bestia, Simulazioni urbane.*

# INDEX

# INDEX

# PHOTO CREDITS

# PHOTO CREDITS

*Cover* ● From left:
*first rank* - Audrey Hepburn; Marilyn Monroe; Marcello Mastroianni.
*second rank* - Clark Gable and Vivienne Leigh; Humprey Bogart; Johnny Deep.

● A playful Shirley MacLaine on a Malibu beach (1956).
*Back Cover* ● From left:
*first rank* - Paul Newman; Sofia Loren; Marlon Brando.
*second rank* - Greta Garbo; Leonardo Di Caprio; Grace Kelly.